I CAN LEARN!

Strategies and Activities for Gray-Area Children

I CAN LEARN!

Strategies and Activities
for Gray-Area Children

GRETCHEN GOODMAN

Crystal Springs Books
Peterborough • New Hampshire

Printed in the United States of America
01 00 99 98 97 96   6 5 4 3 2

Published and distributed by:
Crystal Springs Books
Ten Sharon Road, Box 500
Peterborough, NH 03458-0500
800-321-0401

The pages of this book are printed on recycled paper containing a minimum of 10 percent post-consumer waste.

Publisher Cataloging-in-Publication Data

Goodman, Gretchen, 1952- .
          I can learn! : strategies and activities for gray-area children /
Gretchen Goodman.--1st ed.
[170]p. : ill. ; cm.
Includes bibliography and index.
Summary : Includes ideas for adapting math, reading, writing, handwriting and spelling
activities to fit students' diverse needs. Behavior management strategies and general classroom
adaptations are also provided.
ISBN 1-884548-01-6
1. Remedial teaching. 2. Slow learning children. 3. Teaching. I. Pittet, Phyllis, 1948- .
II. Title.
371.9 / 26--dc20   1995   CIP

Library of Congress number: 95-070936

ISBN 1-884548-01-6
Illustrations and cover design: Phyllis Pittet
Book design: Megan Harrington
Editor: Deborah Sumner

Dedication

This book is dedicated to my daughter Aimee, who has brought me many years of pride, happiness, laughter, and love, and also moments of stress and anxiety and strands of gray hair. She has forced me to be humble in public and has been my safety net to sanity!

Acknowledgments

My husband Harry deserves a special thank you. If he hadn't been running around the country to sporting events, I would have never had a few quiet moments on the computer to write this book. I also want to thank my parents, who will always believe in me; Dr. Barbara Hasson for her advice, encouragement, and support; my TEAM at school; Debbie Sumner for her patience and expertise; my SDE family for giving me so many opportunities; Jim Grant, who insists I always travel with a notepad in hand; and Bubba, my biggest four-legged fan.

Contents

V. Handwriting Adaptations

VI. Spelling Adaptations

VII. Behavioral Management

Introduction — A Teacher's Fairy Tale

Once upon a time in never, never land, where teachers had no lunch duty, bus duty, or recess responsibilities, I began my teaching career. I had a class of 29 first graders in a small classroom without any other adult help. These children all had individual needs and a variety of abilities.

My goal each day was to make sure my students were happy and achieving some kind of success in my class. I spent many hours talking to my friends and colleagues, attempting to devise techniques for providing the children with a challenging, educational environment.

Tim was one of my students. He often reversed his letters and words. Often his name would appear as "MIT." He wrote fat as "taf," bad as "dab," and saw as "was." What was I going to do? Being the warm, caring person I was, I decided I needed to make some adaptations for Tim.

I placed a green dot on the left-hand corner of Tim's desk and a red dot at the right-hand corner. These stop-and-go signals helped Tim remember his directionality. I also marked his reading books with a green arrow at the beginning of each line. Eventually, I stopped marking each line and just marked the top of each page with a green arrow. I also encouraged Tim to practice writing in dry Jell-O in a shoe box lid or with shaving cream on his desk top.

> *"My goal each day was to make sure my students were happy and achieving some kind of success in my class."*

"I thought long and hard about how to help this child be successful in school."

Jennifer also required individual help. She had trouble following directions and completing assigned tasks. I could give the whole group directions, and Jen would forget them by the time she reached her seat. I thought long and hard about how to help this child be successful in school. I knew that she could complete her work if these directions were given to her in bits or chunks, so I developed some adaptations. I placed a tape recorder at the front of the room under my rocking chair when giving whole-group directions. I gave this tape to Jen, so when she returned to her seat she could review lessons and directions. At other times during the day, I gave Jen both written and picture directions. I could inconspicuously hand her an index card with step-by-step direction clues that she could use at her desk as needed. Each time Jen completed tasks on her own, she would cross off that step and then beam with pride.

Then there was Brian! Brian had more energy than the rest of the class combined. All of this excess energy began to interfere with his learning. How could I help this child learn while maintaining my own sanity?

Brian and I sat down and talked. We decided to develop a work contract. Whenever he needed to move around our room, he was able to choose one of his designated "offices" — his own desk, where one part of his body had to touch the chair, a desk with a study carrel for privacy, or a large table at the back of the room where he could spread out his supplies. Our contract stated that Brian had to stay at one of his offices for at least 15 minutes. Brian, his parents, and I signed the contract. Eventually, Brian was able to lengthen the time from 15 to 20 minutes. Once in a while, he made it to 30 minutes.

The adaptations I made in Room 13 allowed the children to progress. Life in first grade moved on until...

The Labeling Begins

Our district began hiring education consultants to help with the Tims, Jens, and Brians. I noticed they would observe my children, mutter some educational jargon, and talk about the need to test some of these children, so we could have an MDE in order to facilitate an IEP and possibly label some children LD or SED.

Imagine how incompetent I felt when talking to these specialists! I had trouble understanding their language and tests. Remember, I was a first-year, first-grade teacher. All I could do was teach!

From the depths of their hearts, these specialists continued to observe, test, classify, and reassign children. Timmy and Jennifer now became LD, and Brian was labeled ADD with an H.

I felt awful! I thought I was meeting my students' needs. Thank goodness these specialists had set me straight. They even offered to take these students out of my room and place them in a secluded classroom at the end of the hall.

Now my only problem was what to do with children between the time of testing and labeling. Certainly they needed to be with a teacher who knew more than I did. I wanted my students to be tested sooner and labeled faster. In the 1970s, more and more children in our school received labels and qualified for special services. These practices continued for the next 10 to 15 years, and then...

The Classroom Teacher's Challenge

Labels became more restrictive; fewer children qualified for special services. Special reading and math programs were phased out of our school. Now what was I to do? I knew I could teach reading, math, and spelling, but could I teach EMR, LD, ADD, Chapter 1, and slow learners?

To this day, teachers all over the nation are faced with the challenge of classrooms which have differently-abled children, children who don't qualify for special education services, and slow learners. Many teachers now receive team-based support, but realize, like I did, that we are once again primarily responsible for meeting the educational needs of all children in our classrooms.

We need to go back to using our former accommodations and strategies developed for the Timmys, Jennifers, and Brians of the school world and know that our efforts will allow all children the opportunity to beam with pride.

That's what this book is for — to share ideas that have worked well with children like Timmy, Jennifer, and Brian.

"...we are once again primarily responsible for meeting the educational needs of all children in our classrooms."

For educators all over the country who say, "If I could only get my hands on one resource book that will give me practical ideas I can implement tomorrow...," this one's for you!

How to Use This Book

I hope this book will help classroom teachers feel comfortable with using in-class adaptations and strategies. *I Can Learn!* includes easy-to-implement, teacher-tested ideas for adapting math, reading, writing, handwriting, and spelling activities to fit students' diverse learning needs. Behavior management strategies and general classroom adaptations are also provided.

Educators from all over the United States have helped develop these ideas, which provide solutions to the challenges we meet daily in our classrooms.

The book is organized by specific areas of the curriculum and can be used by classroom teachers, parents, teaching assistants, peer tutors, and specialists. I advise readers to observe and assess children carefully and develop programs to meet individual needs.

Try several ideas in each section, document what you've tried, and if you discover other successful adaptations, jot down your ideas in the margins. What you learn in working with one child may also help another child later on.

Activities that are particularly well suited for students who learn through auditory, kinesthetic, tactile, or visual modalities will be marked by the following symbols when outlined in black.

 = auditory

 = visual

 = tactile

 = kinesthetic

"I advise readers to observe and assess children carefully and develop programs to meet individual needs."

Activities that are particularly good to use with partners, cooperative learning groups, or small groups are also noted.

= partners

= cooperative learning
(may be partners or groups)

= small groups

Most activities can be adapted for use as needed with individuals, partners, cooperative learning groups, small groups, whole group, or in a learning station.

Some activities can be used for teaching more than one skill. Check the list of activities at the end of some sections for additional possibilities and the skill index in the back of the book.

No activity in this book is only for the at-risk learner. Meaningful hands-on experiences can help all students reach their full learning potential.

"Meaningful hands-on experiences can help all students reach their full learning potential."

I. Who Are the Gray-Area Children?

Gray-area children are sitting in classrooms all across the nation. Teachers often refer to these children as slow learners, at-risk students, or the "tweeners." They qualify for no special education services. Without accommodations made for their particular learning needs, they are in danger of falling between the cracks in the regular classroom.

Gray-area children:

- are commonly known as "the gazers," who can't or won't pay attention.

- may appear to be immature, angry, unsettled, or unfocused, and may require constant redirection or one-to-one supervision.

- fear failure and may refuse to take part in learning.

- often come into our classes hungry, not only for food, but attention.

- may have "invisible disabilities," such as language problems, fetal alcohol syndrome, or attention difficulties.

"Without accommodations made for their particular learning needs, they are in danger of falling between the cracks in the regular classroom."

- perform at a slower pace than most children and require extra wait time.

- usually learn better when shown instead of told and work at a concrete, manipulative stage of development.

- may come to school with extra emotional baggage.

- may move from school to school throughout the year.

- often do not fit in socially with peers, either because of lack of experience or little support from home.

Their classwork may be disorganized, late in arriving, or incomplete. Desks and other belongings often appear to have been shot out of a cannon. They often have their shirt tails out, buttons open, zippers down, and their hair in knots.

It is our challenge as classroom teachers to work with these children, make sure they succeed in school, and help them feel good about themselves each day. We need to adapt existing curriculum, provide strategies that help them learn, and teach them new concepts through concrete, hands-on activities.

I I. General Classroom Adaptations

General Strategies

- Give students hands-on experiences. Use games, learning centers, projects, and speakers in place of worksheets or workbooks.

- Ask yourself, "Will these students need this information five years from now?" If the answer is no, reevaluate the purpose of the instruction.

- Use rebus picture directions.

- Vary tone and pitch of teaching voice.

- Place classroom jobs on individual strips of paper in an empty jar. Students reach in and choose a job to do alone or with a partner.

- Instead of having students constantly raising their hands to respond to questions, vary response modes. For example, students can touch their knees if the answer to 3 x 2 = 5. They may also nod their heads, or cross or uncross ankles to respond.

- Give students work options. "You may do a written end-of-the-chapter sheet or illustrate important events in the chapter."

- To retain important information, kinesthetic learners will often need to do something while restating important facts. Have them snap their fingers, clap their hands, or jump up and down while reciting information such as their phone number, the first ten states, etc.

- Forewarn students of upcoming transitions. Some typical samples might be:

    "We will work on journals for the same amount of time as (name of TV show popular with children)."

    "In five minutes we will begin to clean up centers."

    "In three minutes we will clean up."

    "It is now time to clean up. Let's see if we can be cleaned up by the time we finish singing_____."

- Distribute 3" x 5" index cards to children. One side of the cards says "no" and the other side says "yes." Children flip cards or hold them on their foreheads to respond accordingly.

Developing Self-esteem

- Assist each student with meeting daily success in a variety of settings.

- Provide compliments in a variety of ways.

- Say at least one positive statement to each child daily.

- Give credit for completed work.

- Design "I am special" buttons for each child.

- Chart individual progress.

- Send written "I care" messages to each child daily, or send Happy Gram postcards home to each family at least once a month.

- Build learning expectations upon each learner's strengths.

- Allow students to circle the answers they want checked.

- Mark correct answers only.

- Provide partial credit for work attempted.

Focusing

- Slow the pace of oral directions.

- Limit oral directions. Write directions on the board or overhead to accompany oral directions.

- Give one- or two-step directions at a time. Combine oral with written directions.

- Encourage students to talk themselves through tasks.

- Reduce classroom distractions. Many students are distracted by humming lights and clicking heaters.

- Avoid standing in front of busy, distracting bulletin boards.

- Avoid overdirecting. Use as few words as possible.

- Provide students with page and paragraph number for answers (see pages 112-113).

- Prove the child with a timer to track available time to complete tasks.

- Seat the child close to you during instruction. You may put an "X" on the rug with a specific child's name on it.

- Distribute workbook pages or worksheets one at a time rather than within the whole book. Children will not be distracted by the extra pages.

Organization

- Be consistent so students know what to expect.

- Post a daily schedule visible to all children.

- Make individual "To do" lists (see page 141).

- Chunk assignments and provide directions for small, sequential steps. Instead of giving some children a chapter to read by the end of the week, break it into reasonable bite-size chunks. On Monday read pages 10-14, Tuesday read pages 15-19, Wednesday read pages 20-24, etc.

- Develop individual contracts (see pages 144-145).

- Develop individual goal sheets (see pages 138-140).

- Develop daily assignment books. Have parents or cross-age tutor sign the book on a daily basis.

- Give work samples. Hang a sample of what a completed project or paper should look like.

- Provide word banks on papers (see pages 122-123).

- Seat students in horseshoe format for visual accessibility.

- Enlarge print or spaces on work pages.

Support

- Encourage parent participation in class.

- Provide at-home as well as school copies of texts.

- Check often for understanding.

- Give parents or peer tutors materials to rehearse with students before class.

- Encourage student discussion and collaboration.

- Use peer tutors, cross-age tutors, or study buddies for individual support.

- Allow for extra think time. In advance, give students a written copy of the question(s) you plan to ask them during discussion time.

- Encourage students to orally restate expected tasks to you or to a peer before beginning work.

- Provide immediate oral as well as written feedback.

- Allow for movement and frequent breaks.

- Allow students to take notes for a buddy. Copy your notes for those who are unable to take notes.

- Have more able students tape stories and texts for other classmates to use for rehearsal or as a follow-along activity. This provides auditory along with visual reinforcement. Students are encouraged to start or stop the tape as needed.

- Read tests orally to student.

- Contact a local retirement village for classroom volunteers. A school bus could pick up the retirees in the morning. The volunteers are then assigned a classroom to assist the teacher with projects, paper work, or as a student study buddy. These grandparent volunteers can be treated to a school lunch before riding the bus back to their retirement community.

Developing Self-esteem

 Oral language
Written expression

I Have a Question

Cover an upright tissue box with brightly colored wrapping paper. Place white question marks over the wrapping paper. Leave the tissue slit open at the top of the box. Invite students to use the box as a place for questions they have regarding any school subject. When there is an extra 5-10 minutes of transition time, grab a question and collectively answer it as a class. Some teachers take this a step further and play "Stump the Teacher." Children put their own trivia questions in the box and attempt to stump the teacher whenever there is available time.

 Artistic expression

Where's Waldo?

Using the same format as the popular children's book, give children a small school snapshot of themselves. Have them paste their photos anywhere on a piece of construction paper. Now give children a magazine or catalog and have them cut out pictures. They then place their magazine pictures anywhere on the page while trying to camouflage their own snapshot. The entire class combines their pages together for a fun-filled way to find and identify their hidden friends.

Oral language
Self-assessment

Show Me State(ment)

Instead of using workbooks, written tests, or worksheets, encourage children to involve their classmates with checking for understanding. One child could be in front of a group and say, "Show me two ways to solve 3 x 4" or "Show me two ways to express surprise in written language." This builds individual self-esteem by allowing students to take control of class review and encourages group collaboration.

Developing Self-esteem

Brag Bag

Artistic expression
Oral language
Self-assessment

During the first part of the school year, distribute to each child a large brown paper grocery bag. Invite children to decorate the bag with their names or initials in a creative way (turning letters into animals, initials into logos, etc.). Have children take their bags home and place in them any accomplishments or items they are proud to brag about. Children bring their brag bags to school for sharing time. It's amazing how much background information about children can be gained from this!

Proud Book

Self-assessment

Encourage students to place the work they consider their best effort in a magnetic photo album, along with their name and date. Proud students can gather samples from the month or year and share with visitors.

Look What I Did

Self-assessment

Place a small photo of each student on a classroom bulletin board. Put a push pin under that student's name. When students achieve something they are proud of, it is their very own display place in the room. They are permitted to go to the board and hang work, drawings, kindness statements, etc. (One boy from my pre-first hung his shoe laces there for two weeks after he learned to tie.)

Developing Self-esteem

 Self-assessment

Individual Timelines

Give each class member a prepared timeline for the entire year beginning in September. These individual lines can be hung on a bulletin board or placed inside a manila folder. The timeline is divided into the school months. Allow the child adequate space to write his/her accomplishment for the month.

 Self-assessment

Brag Line

Hang a clothesline across the back of the classroom. At the end of each week, allow students to hang on the line anything they are proud of accomplishing that week. Keep a supply of snap-type clothespins available for children to use. This activity allows them to take ownership for what they have accomplished instead of a teacher-made bulletin board that says, for example, "See the best spellers in Room 23."

 Self-assessment
Written expression

Classroom Timelines

In the front of the classroom, hang a large seasonal shape for that month (September — a large leaf, October — jack o'lantern, etc.). At the end of the month, pass out a 3" x 5" index card to each class member. Encourage students to write whatever important event or accomplishment they remember from the month. All the cards are hung over the seasonal shape and remain up for the year. These memories can then be converted into an end-of-the-year classroom memory book.

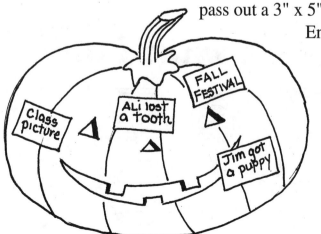

Developing Self-esteem

You Deserve a Hand

Have students trace and cut an outline of their hands and write their names in the center. Pass the hands around the room. Encourage classmates to write a positive statement on each finger. When each finger contains a compliment, return the hand to the owner.

Written expression

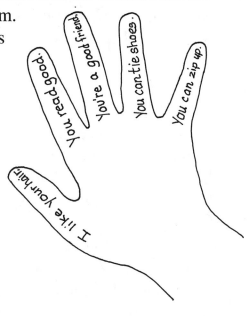

Punch Cards

Place name tags or cut-out animal shapes on students' desks. When you catch students being good, acting appropriately, or completing assigned tasks, punch the card with a hole punch. Design a reward board that might say something such as:

10 punches = lunch with the principal
8 punches = help in kindergarten
5 punches = extra time on the computer

Behavior

Pass the Bag

Have each student decorate a lunch bag. Pass the bag around the classroom to all members of the class. Encourage each student to write a positive statement about that friend and deposit it in the bag. The lunch bags end up with the original owner.

Artistic expression
Written expression

Focusing Strategies

Spotlight

Turn on the overhead projector. Stand in front of the bright light while talking or reading to students. Children who have difficulty focusing will be drawn by the light and will be able to focus on what you say.

**Behavior
Following
  directions
Oral language**

The Ears Have It

Draw a large picture of an ear. Keep this picture under your seat, on the carpet, or in front of the room. When it is necessary for children to really listen to directions or lessons, hold up this ear to help them focus and listen.

This same ear can be used if you are ever faced with a primary class-room of tattlers. Hang an ear picture on a classroom bulletin board. Place a beanbag or rocking chair next to the ear. Encourage children to "tell it to the ear" when they need to tattle.

The Eyes Have It

Before beginning instruction or giving directions, establish eye contact with all students. Verbal cues such as "ready" or "all eyes on me" encourage children to focus on the speaker.

Focusing Strategies

Highlighting Texts

Many students experience success in the classroom by having material in a text highlighted in a consistent fashion. One way to accomplish this is by using blue to highlight definitions, yellow to highlight specific facts, and pink to highlight main ideas. Once the color coding has been established, post a reference chart in the classroom. Share the task of highlighting with colleagues. One teacher could highlight science books for both classes; another could highlight social studies books. Many teachers find that they only have to highlight one or two books each year. This is an excellent way for parents to help.

Organization
Reading
comprehension
  Facts
  Main idea
Study skills
Vocabulary

1 and 2

Make certain that students are focused on the directions. When giving multiple directions, obtain eye contact first. A typical scenario might look like this:

"Please look at me. I'm going to tell you two things to do."

Hold up two fingers.

Touch finger one.

"First, I want you to get out your clay figures."

Pause.

Touch finger two.

"Second, I want you to finish adding the toothpicks."

Following directions

For other focusing ideas, see:

Organizational Strategies

 Number recognition

Tab It

Purchase heavy duty, removable subject tabs. Attach these tabs to pages 10, 20, 30, 40 etc., in a textbook. When students have difficulty getting to the correct page quickly, provide clues such as, "We will be working on page 46. Turn to the 40 tab and find 46 in that section."

IRS Homework Envelopes

Take a large manila envelope. On the outside, write:

Did you remember to write your name? write the date? write the title? use capitals and periods?

The envelope is laminated and students check off their responsibilities in the same fashion as we check off information for the Internal Revenue Service.

Desk Maps

Have students remove all extras from inside their desks, then organize necessary material in corners. Have them draw a map of the desk contents on a 5" x 8" index card. Place the desk map on top of the desk and challenge students to find things in their desk by looking at the map. When a specific article is called, children have until the count of five to retrieve that article without looking inside the desk. With younger children, the desk map can be drawn for them, and they can place items accordingly.

Organizational Strategies

Velcro Schedule

Place a strip of velcro on a student's desk. On 2" squares of paper draw pictures to represent the day's schedule. Place a 1" piece of velcro on back of the schedule cards. Attach pictures to the desk top strip of velcro. Allow the student to move the picture schedule on and off the velcro as the events are completed.

Cut It Out

Workbooks/ worksheets

Use this strategy with students who cannot quickly turn to an assigned page in a consumable workbook. As each page is completed, clip the bottom right-hand corner off the page. When getting ready to find the next page, students put their index finger along the clipped off section and quickly find the next page.

For other organizational ideas, see:

III. Math Adaptations

General Strategies

- Use mini-chalkboards instead of paper and pencil.

- Use sandpaper numbers on flash cards to prevent reversals.

- Encourage children to keep a math dictionary inside their desks. Students can use them if they have difficulty completing worksheets independently.
  Included in this dictionary might be:
    Adding — putting sets together
    Subtracting — taking away from the whole set
    Multiplication — a quick way to add
  Allow children to brainstorm different terms for math operations — regrouping = trading = borrowing = taking from a neighbor.

Math Facts

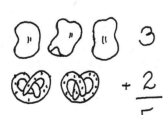

- Practice turning math facts into word problems (see page 45).

- Students manipulate edibles to correspond to facts, then eat their answers (3 chips plus 2 pretzels = 5 treats, yum yum).

Operational Signs

- Provide reference charts for visual clues (+ means add, - means subtract, etc.).

- Highlight or color code operational words in directions and problems.

- Highlight operational signs to lessen confusion (orange for addition, yellow for subtraction). This draws the student's attention to a particular operation. Eventually students will be able to highlight their own operational signs.

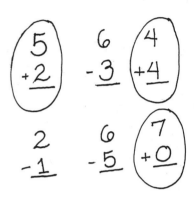

- Cut and paste worksheets to keep all operational signs the same.

- Group problems by similarities in wording and operation.

- Place circles or boxes around problems with similar operational signs. This draws the student's eye to a particular type of problem.

- Provide stop signs on the page at the end of the rows if the operations change with each row.

- Use glitter glue to highlight specific signs for children. This provides tactile as well as visual clues.

- Use separate paper for each type of mathematical operation. Some children may need to have these separate papers color coded for operational ease. (Often a 5th- or 6th-grade tutor or parent volunteer can do this at home.)

Workbooks/Worksheets

- Cut worksheet into strips to avoid overwhelming students. Distribute strips after each is completed.

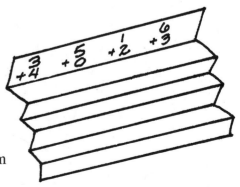

- Fold worksheets or tests into fans. This minimizes the amount of work the student sees at one time.

- Give fewer problems and more time for completion.

- Arrange problems from easiest to hardest and separate them with a dark black line.

- Provide plenty of work space on math papers.

- Provide answer banks at the top of a page.

- Provide multiple choice answers.

- Have students solve half of the problems independently and use a calculator for the rest.

- Assign only odd-numbered problems to be completed.

- Provide answer keys on the back of the papers for self-checking.

- Allow students to choose the problems they will complete and circle the ones they want corrected.

- Read word problems silently, then orally to identify and highlight difficult words.

- Turn lined paper horizontally for number placement.

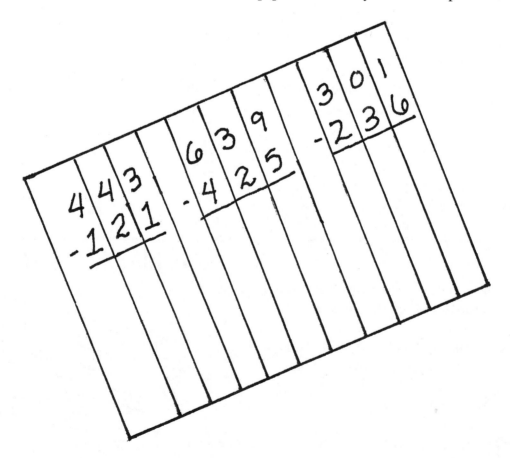

Division

First Numeral

Ask the student who is unable to complete long division problems to solve and find only the first or first and second numerals in the quotient. Given the problem 81453 divided by 9, some may only solve 81 divided by 9 and then stop.

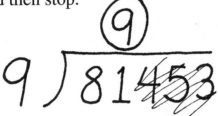

Short of Long Division

When providing children with clues for long division, hang a reference chart that states the steps necessary for completing long division.

1) Divide
2) Multiply
3) Subtract
4) Bring it down
5) Check your answer

The Cheese Burger Trick

When applying the above steps for long division, teach students the following auditory aid: Does McDonald's sell cheeseburgers? Or,

d = divide
m = multiply
s = subtract
c = compare
b = bring down

Number recognition

Organization

Organization

Fractions

Real-life Learning

Children are more comfortable with fraction problems if they have been allowed to work with concrete objects. Have them cut a cookie in half. One child cuts and the other child chooses the half s/he wants. This encourages children to cut equally in half. Pizza parties and sandwich swaps encourage use of fractional parts.

Number Lines

Fraction number lines are helpful to children who cannot visualize part and whole. The fraction number line may be kept on individual desks for use on an as needed basis.

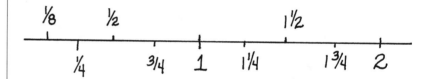

Color coding

Many times children need to refer to a color-coded chart kept in the room for easy reference or to a desk top chart to refresh their thinking as to which part of the fraction is the numerator or denominator.

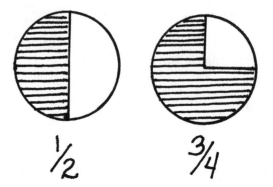

Math Facts

Addition/Subtraction

Manipulatives

Place the addition fact you would like completed on a separate piece of paper. Give the student counters to be placed directly next to the numerals. Now allow the student to move the counters directly to the answer spot. This final step of moving the manipulatives reinforces the joining of sets.

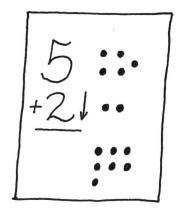

Moving Flash Cards

Give the child the specified math fact on a flash card that has a hole punched at the bottom and a shoelace or string attached. Encourage children who need manipulatives to string beads, macaroni, or Cheerios to match the facts and check their work.

Self-assessment

Walking Number Lines

At the front of the room, have a walkable number line ready for children. (Make sure to leave enough room in between the numerals for wheelchairs and walkers.) Use 2-inch wide masking tape for the line and numerals. (This makes it quick and easy to take apart.) Encourage students to walk or jump their problems as they would with individual desk number lines.

Math Facts

Desk Lines

Students of all ages may need to rely on a desk number line at some time. Often parents will ask how to use the number line when teaching addition, so a transportable one for school and home is helpful. (Many parents aren't aware that they can simply use a ruler as a number line to solve simple problems.) Teach parents and students how to look at simple problems such as 4 + 5. Place a finger on the first number in the problem (4). Have students locate that number on the number line and "hop" forward 5 more to get the answer. The reverse is used for subtraction. To solve 10 - 2, have students start at the first number on the number line (10) and "jump" backwards 2 places.

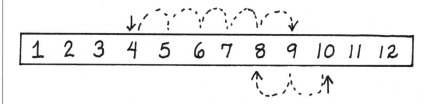

Finger Clues

Give the child a problem such as 9 + 3. Put a line through the first number (9). Place three fingers in the air. Begin counting those fingers with the number after 9 (10, 11, 12). When the child has no more fingers left up, the last number stated is the answer (12).

Doubles

Some children are more successful learning math facts with the doubles trick. Providing them with reference charts may make learning addition facts easier, especially if they need to see the "how" of the solution. If the problem is 5 + 6, encourage the child to think of the smaller number in the problem (5). Put a box around that number and double it (10). Remind the child that 6 is one more than 5 so s/he can add one more to find the answer (11). This same procedure can be used for a number that is two more than the double. For example, 5 + 7 — the child doubles the 5 (10) and adds 2.

Number Bear, Number Bear

Using a familiar chant from children's literature, teach students facts such as: "10 Bear, 10 Bear what do you see?" "I see 7 + 3 equal to me." Bears and matching number facts can be paired up for this game.

Jumping Math Facts

Using a jump rope or small trampoline, one student reads a flash card to another. The first student jumps the numbers on the card while his/her helper counts the total number of jumps. Students check each other by looking at the correct answer on the reverse side of the card.

Self-assessment

Math Facts

Headband Facts

Purchase two inexpensive terry cloth headbands. Have two students put on headbands. Give each student an index card with a numeral on it. Without looking at the numeral, the child places it in the headband. Both students face each other. The teacher calls out the sum of the two numerals. While looking at the other child's numeral, each child tries to figure out what is in his/her own headband. The first child who gives the correct answer wins.

Dot-to-Dots

Give the student math flash cards. S/he arranges already prepared glitter glue dot cards over the flash cards and counts and touches while completing the addition facts.

Dice ("random number generators")

Have a student roll two dice. Next s/he adds or subtracts the number combination which appears. A third die that has an operational sign on it may be used. With young children, foam bricks cut from upholstery foam work best and are more easily manipulated by little hands. Use an electric knife to cut the foam and wide permanent marker to write the numerals.

Math Facts

Multiplication/Division

Circle sets

When giving the problem 9 divided by 3, have the student draw nine dots and divide them into sets of three. Or, give the child nine blocks and have him or her arrange them into sets of three.

Multiplication Grids

Provide students with manipulative number grids and indexes which they can use in pairs or alone to review and check for mastery. Both the grids and index cards are on separate paper.

Self-assessment

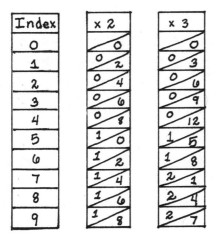

Index	x 2	x 3
0	0	0
1	0 2	0 3
2	0 4	0 6
3	0 6	0 9
4	0 8	0 12
5	1 0	1 5
6	1 2	1 8
7	1 4	2 1
8	1 6	2 4
9	1 8	2 7

Simplifying Multiplication Facts

Teach the student how to simplify the number of facts needed to memorize.

0 x any = 0
1 x any = any
2 x any = any doubled
5 x any = Count to any by 5 (5 x 3 = 5, 10, 15)

Math Facts

Finger Multiplication for 9's

Students who experience difficulty with memorization may need to rely on finger facts for 9's. Teach them to put up both hands. If the problem to be solved is 3 x 9, have them begin with the left-hand pinky finger, count 3, and put down the finger that was counted as number 3. The number of fingers standing to the left of 3 are counted as tens (2) and the number to the right of the bent finger are counted as ones (7).

9's Trick

Subtract 1 from the multiplier to obtain the tens column, add enough to that numeral to make 9 for the ones column. (9 x 7 = 7 - 1 = 6 for the tens column, and 6 + 3 = 9 for the ones column, thus 63)

Flipping Cards

Flipping flash cards are used to help students learn multiplication facts. Use index cards and brass brads. If students are having trouble with 3 x 2, design the cards to look like this:

Math Facts

100s Chart

Color code a laminated hundreds chart for the desired skill. When teaching the 2's table, color code the numbers, counting by two.

Multiplication Charts

Have a multiplication chart made out of sturdy oaktag available for any students who choose to use one. Demonstrate how children can use rubberbands or yarn to keep their place on the chart and find their answer where the two numbers intersect.

1	2	3	4	5	6	7	8	9	10	11	12
2	4	6	8	10	12	14	16	18	20	22	24
3	6	9	12	15	18	21	24	27	30	33	36
4	8	12	16	20	24	28	32	36	40	44	48
5	10	15	20	25	30	35	40	45	50	55	60
6	12	18	24	30	36	42	48	54	60	66	72
7	14	21	28	35	42	49	56	63	70	77	84
8	16	24	32	40	48	56	64	72	80	88	96
9	18	27	36	45	54	63	72	81	90	99	108
10	20	30	40	50	60	70	80	90	100	110	120
11	22	33	44	55	66	77	88	99	110	121	132
12	24	36	48	60	72	84	96	108	120	132	144

Math Facts

Self-assessment

Self-assessment

All Operations

Trace and Learn

The child traces four math facts to learn on tracing paper. These four math facts must be traced at least three times each. The child should whisper or say each fact into a tape recorder as s/he writes it. The child then prints the four facts from memory on white paper. Have a study buddy write the facts on index cards and double check for mastery. Any that are missed should be repeated on the tracing paper.

Tape Recorder Facts

On a blank tape, record math problems slowly and clearly. The child stops the tape, writes the facts, solves the problem, and turns the tape back on for a private self-check.

Mathematical Baseball

Draw a large baseball diamond on the chalkboard. Write three sets of numbers beside home plate, first base, second, and third. The pitcher's mound receives the multiplier or addend. Each player must complete the assigned problem before moving to the next base.

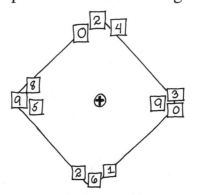

Math Facts

Pocket Math

Have 10 library cards glued on oaktag. Write the numerals 1-10 on each card. Place math facts on index cards. Students must match cards to the correct pocket. Answers are on the back of the card for self-checking.

Auditory Reinforcement

Many students with a strong auditory preference recall math facts better when they hear them aloud. Use a Language Master for auditory reinforcement. Allow children to actually look at the answer side of the flash card while reading the problem and saying the answer into the Language Master. Others are then able to listen to the facts. Students can bounce balls or clap patterns as they practice these facts.

Slides

Purchase blank slides from a camera shop. Use a projector pen to write a problem on one slide and the answer on the next. The slide projector can then be set on a carousel timer. Facts are flashed on the board and students write their answers and check them when the answer slide is flashed on. In addition to providing a fun-filled way to review, students are also provided with large muscle activities of writing on the board.

Math Facts

Number Films

Use old lamination strips from the recycling bin to make your own filmstrips. Cut the lamination strips the same size as a filmstrip and run the strips through the projector with math facts on them.

Reading comprehension
Sight words
Spelling
Written expression

Flim Flam Film

To make instant filmstrips, dip old out-of-date filmstrips in a mixture of $1/4$ cup bleach and two cups of water to remove the color. Use these filmstrips for math facts, reading, or turning student stories into movies.

Geometric shapes
Operations

Concentration Math

This game is played exactly like the old TV show. Use 20 index cards. Depending on the concept that needs reinforcement, make card pairs such as math facts and answers, geometric shapes and names, or mathematical symbols and definitions. Randomly mix the cards, four cards to five rows. Children turn two cards over at a time while attempting to correctly match the cards. (Color code problems by using white index cards for the problems and yellow index cards for the answers.)

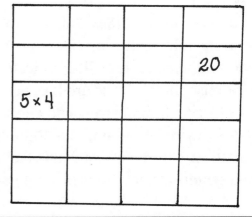

Math Facts

Dialing for Math Facts

Cut out a large circular phone dial (or collect discarded phones from the phone company). One child dials a single number of his/ her choice. The next child dials his/her favorite number. The two must follow the operational sign in the middle of the dial and complete the problem together.

Fact Ferris Wheel

Cut out a 6-inch circle. Decorate the outside edges to resemble a ferris wheel. Write a numeral on each of the seats. Place an arrow in the middle of the circle. See how quickly students can get around the edges of the wheel. Children can be given a ferris wheel to match their individual levels of performance.

Bean Bag Math

Use masking tape to section a portion of the floor into 12 segments. Students take turns tossing a bag into a square and completing the problem there. (Problems can be written on a 5" x 8" index card taped into the square.)

Musical Math Chairs

This game is played exactly like musical chairs. However, there is a laminated math card problem on each seat. When the music stops, students claim seats, but must complete the problem to remain in that chair.

Math Facts

Kinesthetic Facts

Encourage students to jump, tap, or use cheering pom-poms to chant their multiplication, addition, subtraction, or division facts.

Number recognition

Beach Ball Fun

Use a large segmented beach ball to help students "catch" their facts. Write a numeral on each segmented section. Before tossing the ball to a student, state the operation to be used, such as subtraction. After the student catches the ball, s/he must subtract the two numbers hiding under his/her thumbs. Beachball math can also help students with number recognition.

Bingo

Many elementary students enjoy the reinforcement of number bingo. The teacher is able to make grid cards for the entire class that have the answers randomly place at different locations. Children work in pairs. The teacher calls out number facts such as 7 - 5 or 6 + 8, and children cover the correct answer location on their grid. Allowing children to work in pairs while using number lines or manipulatives will help them learn math in a more concrete way.

For other math facts activities, see:
Twister Math, p. 33
Yarn Ball Review, p. 80
Paint Bags, p. 81

Number Recognition

Twister Math

Use an old shower curtain, tablecloth, or twister game for this activity. Cover the cloth or game sheet with numbers that children are reviewing. For some children, the direction card may simply be, "Put a foot on number 3 and a hand on 7." For older children, the direction card may be, "Put a right foot on 3 and a left foot on 9. Multiply the numbers and tell your partner the answer."

**Math facts
Following directions**

Tip-Tap Numbers

Have each child write each numeral 1-10 on separate 3-inch squares. Using a xylophone, tap out a specific number of tones. The child then holds up a corresponding number card.

For other number recognition activities, see:

Tab It, p. 14
First Numeral, p. 19
Beach Ball Fun, p. 32
Who's in Place, p. 35
Place It, p. 35
Read My Mind, p. 36
Ring It, p. 36
Flipping for Places, p. 37
Place Value Doilies, p. 37
Abacus, p. 37
Thumb Tracers, p. 40
Canvas Charts, p. 41
Water Painting, p. 42
Overhead Math, p. 42
Dot-to-Dots, p. 42
Pit Bull Role Play, p. 43
Paint Bags, p. 81
Back Writing, p. 93
Rainbow Letters, p. 126

One-to-One Correspondence

Matching One-to-One

1. Have children pass straws, napkins, or pencils, matching one to one.

2. Ring a desk top bell and have children make tally marks to correspond one to one.

3. Play musical chairs.

4. Count slowly as a class to see how high children can count until everyone is buttoned and zipped.

5. Blow up real balloons and match strings to balloons.

6. Melt chocolate and match lollipop sticks to each chocolate shape.

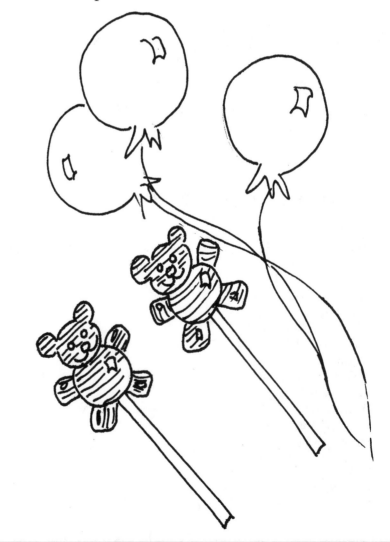

Place Value

Who's in Place?

Distribute numerals (0 to 9) to the children. On three separate sheets of paper, write the words hundreds, tens, and ones. Place these sheets on the floor and call out a particular number, such as 342. The child holding a 3 stands on the hundreds sheet, the child with a 4 stands on the paper labeled tens, and the child with a 2 stands on the ones paper. With those three children, the numbers can be mixed up again — 423 — to further check for understanding.

Place It

On the front board, write the words hundreds, tens, and ones in large letters. Distribute individual 0-9 numeral cards to children. Call out a specific number such as 985. Have children go to the front of the room and place their cards in the correct spot.

Manipulatives

Use beads, straws, paper clips, or Tinkertoys (10 holes in the round connectors) for place value. Students will have hands-on experience with filling places in groups of 10 and moving to the next place.

Place Value

Organization

**Number
  recognition**

**Letter recognition
Number
  recognition
Numeral formation
Reversals**

Graphs

Provide the student with clear acetate overlays which graph the place value of specific problems. Or, label his/her work in graph box columns — hundreds, tens, ones, etc. Use ½-inch graph paper to line up problems or numerals in the correct place.

				1	6	9
				2	8	8
				h	t	o

Ring It

Using plastic spirals for binding, hook together three different colored index cards. (You could also use metal ring binders on a dowel rod.) All cards are numbered 0-9. The person in charge calls out a number such as 789, and children flip their individual cards to form that number. This activity could also be done on the tape recorder and used at a learning center while other children are completing a different math task.

Read My Mind

Children cover their desks or table tops with shaving cream. The teacher explains that it is now their job to read the teacher's mind. S/he describes a number and children write it on their desk tops. For example, "I am thinking of a number that has 7 hundreds, 5 tens, and 6 ones. Write that number if you can read my mind." (Shaving cream also helps clean dirty desks.)

As a variation of this game, children can shape the number out of play dough, or write it in pudding, dry Jell-O, sand, salt, or on fingerpaint bags (see page 81). This activity can also be adapted to reinforce number or letter recognition and help children who have reversal problems with numbers, letters, or words.

Place Value

Flipping for Places

Each group of four students receives a 12" x 18" piece of oaktag divided into thirds. Label the sections hundreds, tens, and ones. One child flips the tiddlywinks, nine in all. The chips should fall in either the hundreds, tens, or ones place. One child calls out the number formed by the toss of the chips. Another child writes the number and the fourth child checks the response and cleans the board. Children switch roles for the next turn.

Number recognition
Numeral formation

hundreds	tens	ones
• • • •	• • •	• •

432

Place Value Doilies

Give each student four or five paper doilies with a variety of five- or six-digit numbers on them. The teacher has a duplicate set. The teacher calls out 4-7-6-4-3. The child holding that doily replies, "I have forty-seven thousand, six hundred, forty three." The child who correctly identifies all his/her numerals becomes the teacher.

Number recognition

Abacus

Have your school's industrial arts class make large, labeled abacuses for children who need manipulatives for place value. For example, take a piece of wood and attach dowel rods that are labeled **th**, **h**, **t**, and **o**. Give the child a numeral card with colored place value numbers and request that s/he place the colored beads on the abacus to correspond with the place value of numerals on the card.

Number recognition

Regrouping

Boxes

Teach students to place boxes above and below math problems to provide visual clues for where to place numbers that are regrouped. Some numbers may need to be provided students in the beginning, but such clues will eventually be eliminated.

$$\begin{array}{r} \boxed{1} \\ 62 \\ +\ 19 \\ \hline 1 \end{array}$$

Carry Underneath

Many children are more successful with addition regrouping when they can carry numbers under the problem, where they can more easily visualize the steps.

$$\begin{array}{r} 62 \\ 19 \\ \hline \boxed{1} \\ 81 \end{array}$$

Talking

Many times auditory learners are able to talk themselves through a problem and understand the concept of borrowing or carrying. "Okay, 4 + 9 is 13. Put down 3 ones. Carry 1 ten over to the tens column. Now, 7 + 5 is 12 and one more makes 13."

$$\begin{array}{r} 1 \\ 74 \\ +59 \\ \hline 3 \end{array}$$

Regrouping

Color Coding

Use color-coded signs (red and green) to emphasize working problems from right to left.

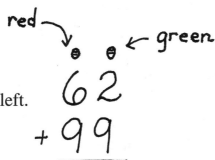

Workbooks/
worksheets

Visuals

Provide children with a sample reference chart, on worksheets or at the front of the room, which walk them through the regrouping process with written explanations of each step involved.

Organization
Workbooks/
worksheets

Regrouping With Addition:

- Add the ones (6 + 9)
- Is it bigger than 10? (15 — yes)
- Put the ones in the ones place (5)
- Carry the 1 ten (from 15) to the tens place
- Add the tens (1 + 2 + 8)
- Put your answer (11)

$$\begin{array}{r} {}^{1}26 \\ +\ 89 \\ \hline 115 \end{array}$$

Regrouping With Subtraction:

- Start in the ones place
- If the bottom number is bigger than the top (9 is bigger than 1)
- Borrow one ten from the tens place
- Show where you borrowed
- Place the 1 ten in front of the ones place
- Subtract the bottom number (11 - 9 = 2)
- Subtract the tens place (5 - 2)

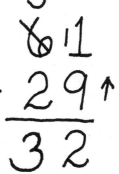

39

Reversals

Numeral formation
Numeral recognition

Thumb Tracers

Have students trace the outline of their left hand. Using this outline, they will be able to talk themselves through numeral shapes.

• Number 1 is straight down from index to thumb.

• Number 2 curves around the index toward the inner part of the thumb and straight out.

• Number 3 is around the thumb and back again.

• Number 4 is made by holding the hand straight up, fingers together. Come straight down next to the index, across the top of the thumb, lift and go back down the other side and straight down.

• Number 5 is begun like 4. Come straight down past the index and around the thumb to form a curve, putting a lid on at the end.

• Number 6 is made with the C, starting at the index, curving around the inner circle of the thumb and looping back in.

• Number 7 comes across the thumb and down.

• Number 8 is formed by opening the fingers and starting at the index finger and forming a C over the thumb. Children curve under the thumb to make it look like an S, cross on top of the thumb, and hook on top.

• Number 9 begins the same way as an 8 by forming the C, but curves back toward the index and straight down. (Students will enjoy having a reference chart to model, tracing each other's hands, or using an Ellison machine hand cutouts.)

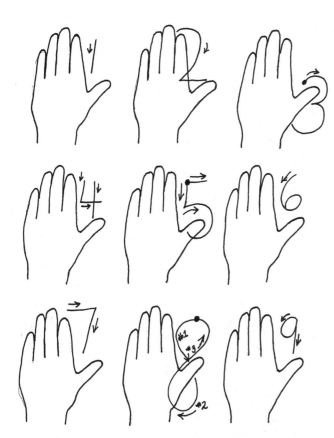

Reversals

Screen Boards

Use a 12" x 18" piece of plywood or the bottom of a soda case. Cover the left half of it with acetate or a piece of old lamination. Make sure that the left-hand edge is not taped down since this is where a piece of paper will be slipped under. Cover the other side of the board with screening or rug canvas. This piece gets taped to the piece of lamination. Place a correct model of a letter, numeral, or word underneath the lamination. Have the student trace over the model with a wipe-off pen. Next, the student traces on a piece of paper placed over the screen. If the student uses a thick crayon, the numeral will have a raised effect for future tracing. Students can also use the screen board to reinforce correct spelling and review sight words.

Letter formation
Numeral formation
Sight words
Spelling

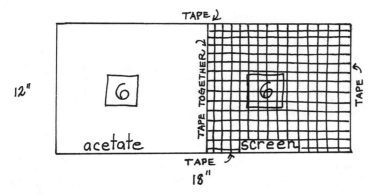

Canvas Charts

Have students trace numbers over needlepoint or rug canvas. The correct model of the numeral can be placed underneath the canvas while the student traces on top with an index finger. Students can place a piece of white paper over the canvas and use crayons to trace numerals on the paper. Be certain students have a model to copy. The raised effect made with crayons on white paper over the canvas offers a lasting tactile impression for children. They can also practice letter formation this way.

Letter formation
Letter recognition
Numeral formation
Numeral recognition

Reversals

Letter formation
Letter recognition
Numeral formation
Number
  recognition
Sight Words
Spelling

Letter formation
Letter recognition
Numeral formation
Number
  recognition
Sight words
Spelling

Numeral formation
Number
  recognition

Water Painting

Allow children to have 3-inch paint brushes and water buckets. They paint large numerals on the chalkboard or playground using peer partners for checking. (This activity can also be used to practice writing letters, sight words, or spelling.)

Overhead Math

Have large numerals printed on an overhead transparency. Children trace them as they are projected onto the chalkboard or large white chart paper. (Also, children can practice writing letters, sight words, or spelling.)

Dot-to-Dots

Teachers can make raised dot charts of numerals with drops of glue or glitter-glue pens. Children trace dot-to-dot to form numerals.

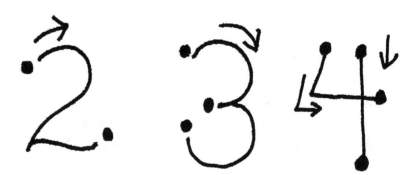

For other reversal prevention activities, see:
Read My Mind, p. 36
Paint Bags, p. 81
Rainbow Letters, p. 126

Rounding Off

Pit Bull Role Play

Place a cutout of a large house at the front of the room. Label this 200 Park Avenue. At the right, label another house 300 Park Avenue. Choose one child to be Mikey and another to be the pit bull. Tell the group that Mikey lives at 200 Park Avenue. His best friend Tina lives at 300 Park Avenue. One day Mikey decides to get up enough nerve to take a bunch of flowers to Tina. He goes out 200 Park Avenue and gets to 230 when a vicious pit bull charges after him. Is Mikey safer to run back to 200 or go on to 300? Through repeated dramatization, students internalize the concept of rounding off by visually deciding which number is closest to the hundreds place.

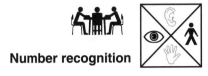

Number recognition

Time

Organization

Time is Relative

Tape individual clocks onto students' desks. Relate time to everything. Say, "Set your clock for thirty minutes from now. That's when we will stop journal writing." Or say, "When the big hand gets on the 12, we'll leave for recess. Set your clocks accordingly."

When teaching students how to tell time, the best sequence is hour, half-hour, quarter-hour, five minutes before and after the hour, then minutes and seconds.

Self-assessment

Wrap Around the Clock

Use a tape measure segmented into increments of five and stretch it around a clock dial. This gives children a visual image of five-minute intervals. Have a digital clock available for children to self-check their individual clock time.

Human Clocks

Show children a given time or state one. They set their arms to read like the clock would. Or, have clock numerals placed on the floor in a large circle. Have one child be the short hand and another be the long hand. The class decides on a time, and the two children must lie in the center of the circle and point themselves to the correct numerals to make that time.

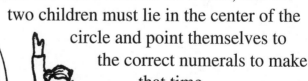

Word Problems

Real Stories

Allow children to make up their own stories using information that relates to them. By giving children a guide for word problems, they are able to compose their own stories and share them with friends.

Sample: Aimee had four jelly beans. She gave two to Bubba. How many jelly beans did she have left?

Written expression

Oral Reading

Often students will need to hear a word problem read to them or dramatized in order to conceptualize the facts and operations needed. Classmates can work together in pairs or cross-age tutors can work together (for example, a 10-year-old can assist a 6-year-old).

Reading Level

Many times the reading level of word problems is so complex that students are unable to perform the necessary steps. White out the unnecessary words that may slow down some students; highlight or box key operational words in written problems (in all, altogether, are left). Read problems out loud and then encourage students to state or rewrite the problem in their own words.

Focusing
Oral language

Word Problems

Artistic expression
Focusing
Oral language
Organization

Walking Through a Word Problem

1. Allow the student time to read the word problem.

2. Have the student describe in his/her own words what happened and the setting.

3. Ask "What is the problem asking you to do?"

4. Discuss mathematical steps needed to solve the problem.

5. Highlight key words such as "in all," "are left," "remaining," etc.

6. Estimate what the answer might be, how it will look in relation to the other numbers.

7. Illustrate the problem if necessary.

This adaptation works well with peer partners, cross-age tutors, or parent volunteers.

Operational signs
Organization
Workbooks/
  worksheets
Written expression

Writing Word Problems

Read the problems out loud. Have students clap when you come to the operational sign. Or, have them stand up if they need to add, or touch their toes if they should subtract.

Tie math into whole language by having children write their own workbooks instead of purchasing workbooks. Provide a skeletal outline of words to be used.

_____ had _____.
a friend   how many things

_____ had _____.
a friend   how many things

How many in all?

_____ had _____.
a name   number things

_____ gave _____ away.
she/he   number

How many are left?

IV. Reading and Writing Adaptations

General Strategies

- Using the same format as a general interest survey, survey pupils about reading preferences. This survey can be read to younger children. It can be shared with parents and kept as part of the running portfolio. Some typical questions at the elementary level might be:

  Who is your favorite author? Where do you like to read? Do you have a library card? Do you learn more from pictures or words?

- Instill in all children the motto, "Be the best reader and writer you can be."

- Encourage reading in a variety of settings — old sofas, clawfoot bathtubs, car seats.

  - Make literature fun, not work.

    - Encourage students to read to a pet or stuffed animal.

    - Relate real-life experiences to reading.

Adaptations

- Allow for longer think and process time.

- Encourage shared reading with partners or triads. Provide extra adults for book sharing time.

- Check the size of print in reading books.

- Provide the reader with comprehension questions before reading.

- Make literature available on tape for auditory learners.

- Provide puzzles, games, and hands-on centers for review.

- Read into the student's ear while s/he reads out loud.

- Instead of assigning all students a written report, allow children the opportunity to choose whether they prefer to do an illustration, a collage, or an oral report.

- Consistently provide auditory along with visual interactions with literature.

Develop Assessment Skills

- Develop observation skills to note individual needs, weaknesses, and strengths.

- Provide quick feedback through individual reading/writing conferences. Help children see and record their own progress.

- Help children develop self-assessment and peer-sharing skills.

- In order to demonstrate individual growth, tape record each student's reading once a month. Children can be allowed to visit the tape center individually once they've mastered the taping technique. Older students can assist in this process also. Many parents willingly send audio tapes to school to help preserve this priceless memory.

- Videotape students once a month if you have the equipment. This not only shows reading progress, but provides a visual document that reflects individual growth while interacting with the written word.

Provide a Print-rich Environment

- Provide plenty of time for exploration of books and literature.

- Find out children's interests and tap into them.

- Help children become more worldly in their knowledge by providing them with a variety of experiences.

- Have available a wide range of reading materials for students to explore.

- Provide high-interest materials.

Dot-to-Dot Newspapers: ABC Order

To reinforce alphabet sequence, give students a section of a newspaper. Ask them to find the first A they see. From this point they are to draw a line to a B, then find a C, etc. Ask them to imagine/identify what their dot-to-dot picture will resemble when completed.

Alphabetical order
Letter recognition

Working Letters

Write one letter of the alphabet on index cards and distribute a card to each student. Assign a variety of tasks for each day of the week.

For example:

On Monday, write a tongue twister with the letter chosen from the pile.

On Tuesday, form a letter collage using alphabet pictures from a magazine.

On Wednesday, write your letter in Braille.

On Thursday, turn your new letter into an animal.

On Friday, list foods from each food group that begin with that letter.

Artistic expression
Letters/sounds
Written expression

Word Pockets

Glue 26 library pockets on a piece of poster board. Write a letter of the alphabet on each pocket. Place index cards in each pocket. Encourage children to write the words they learned beginning with that letter on one line of the card. As others need help writing or reading those words, they are allowed to visit the pocket for the correct spelling.

Alphabetical order
Letters/sounds
Sight words
Spelling

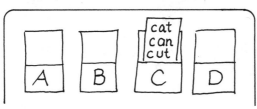

Alphabet

Alphabetical order
Letter recognition

Alphabetical order
Decoding
Letter recognition
Letters/sounds
Spelling
Vowels

Letter formation
Letter recogniton

ABC Line Up

Distribute individual letters to small groups of students. On the count of three, children line up in correct alphabetical order as quickly as possible.

Rug Reading

Collect rug samples from a local furniture store. Using 18-inch stencils, spray paint a letter of the alphabet on each rug. Children can use the rugs to walk the alphabet, skip over vowels, sit with friends on words they've put together, etc.

Human Alphabet

Have children work in pairs or triads and use their bodies to form capital letters. Teachers can stand on a desk and photograph the human letters. These photos are then hung up with the class alphabet.

For another alphabet activity, see:
Alphabet Cereal, p. 78

Alternatives to Book Reports

Dying to Read and Write

Artistic expression
Oral language
Written expression

Cut a square piece of foam from an upholstery form. Cover each side of the die with sunshine faces numbered from 1 to 6. On a separate piece of paper, write numbers 1-6 and a variety of ways students can choose to report on their readings. A student tosses the cube and refers to the paper for the assigned method of reporting.

Student Choice

Artistic expression
Oral language
Reading
comprehension
  Main idea
Sequence
Written expression

Instead of written book reports, have a child:
- act out a phone conversation with the main character
- draw a mural to depict the main idea
- cut and paste sentence strips that represent correct sequence
- make newspaper headlines to support the main idea
- write a letter to the main character
- illustrate a poster to advertise the book
- dress up in costume as the main character
- videotape a TV commercial advertising why someone else should purchase the book
- make greeting cards for the author
- make a billboard advertisement for the book
- develop a comic strip to depict the main events or a different ending
- design an original book jacket for the literature s/he has read or heard

Alternatives to Book Reports

It's Party Time

Upon competing a particular trade book, invite students to list ten birthday presents they would send to the main character or to a supporting character.

Oral language

Picture This

Have students cut and paste three magazine pictures that resemble the main character from a story or the main problem in a story. They need to orally explain how the magazine picture resembles elements from the story.

Artistic expression

Report Envelopes

Give each student a 6" x 9" clasp manila envelope. The student first decorates the front of the envelope with a scene from the story. The title and author are clearly written on the front of the envelope. The student then takes a piece of 9" x 12" oaktag and illustrates a favorite scene from the story. The picture is laminated and then cut apart to make a puzzle. The puzzle pieces are put inside the envelope and passed around the room for peers to assemble.

Alternatives to Book Reports

Building a Story Frame

Older students may sometimes need a frame of reference to use for writing a book report. Allowing them to have this before reading the selection often eases problem with writing the report.

The name of the book was _____

_____ .

The problem faced by the main character was _____ .

The way everything worked out was _____ .

If I could call someone from the story it would be _____ .

The words I would like to say to the author are _____ .

Compound Words

Teamwork

Group students into two teams. Each member of the team is given a word. The students must pair themselves up with someone on the other team to make a compound word. For younger children, this can be simplified by having the words written on half a geometric shape. Children then match shapes to discover what word they have made.

Chain 'Em Up

Students are given pieces (1" x 4") of a paper chain. They must combine the word written on their chain with another student's word to form a compound word. Some students are able to take blank chains and write their own words to form compounds.

Beam Me Up

Using a classroom balance beam (or a taped line on the floor), have children line up at opposite ends of the beam holding given words, such as dog and house. These two children simultaneously walk onto the beam and join in the center to form the new word.

Sailing Away

Cut out the bottom of a sailboat and two sails. Have the child join the two sails together that would form a compound word and attach them together on the boat. The child writes the newly formed compound word on the bottom of the boat.

For another compound words activity, see:

Check-up Checkers, p. 94

Comprehension

Where Is It?

When giving students comprehension questions, provide the page number where they can locate the answer. Take this a step further by placing a colored dot after the question and the same colored dot next to the paragraph where the answer can be found.

Prereading Strategies

Allow children time to picture read. Guidance from the teacher might include:

Look at the picture.
- When does this story take place? What time of day is it? Year?
- Can you tell who some of the main characters of the story might be from the picture?
- How does this picture make you feel? How might the people in the story be feeling?

Look at a given page.
- Find the word "little." Find a period. Count the question marks. What was the first word on the page? The last?
- Find a word that starts with p. Find one that means the same as short. Find a boy's name.

Now, read the story.

Focusing
Organization

King/Queen of the Hill

Have a student sit on a designated "throne." Other students attempt to knock the king/queen off the seat with questions about content or comprehension. If questions are not answered, the person is dethroned and the challenger becomes the king/queen.

Oral language

Comprehension

Artistic expression
Focusing
Oral language
Self-assessment
Written expression

Comprehension Strategies

1. Have students use a telephone to call the main character from the book to discuss the story's outcome or a possible new plot.

2. Develop a letter to the main character of the story supporting an action that took place.

3. After reading a book, have the student compose a telegram stating the main events or beginning, middle, ending events in the story. Limit the size of the telegram.

4. Encourage students to understand why they are reading something before they begin to read.

5. Encourage predictions during the story. Write down the predictions and place them in a hat. Choose a few to discuss after reading.

6. Allow for self-discussion during reading — "What did I learn and how will I use this new material?"

7. When provided with specific questions from a peer or teacher about a story:
   • read the question to yourself or a peer tutor;
   • turn the question into part of your oral or written answer;
   • find the answer in the material; and
   • complete the answer.

8. Provide multiple choice comprehension questions. (Often it may be necessary for the teacher to provide one correct answer for every two obviously incorrect answers until the student becomes comfortable with the process.) Provide comprehension hints to less obvious questions if needed.

Comprehension

Moving Picture Books

To encourage children to read, allow them to bring in four or five photographs from home (or use classroom photos). Use glue to attach the pictures on a long strip of oaktag. Fold a 12" x 18" paper in half, cut a hole out of the center, and cover the hole with clear acetate. This hole now resembles a TV screen. The picture frames should be able to slide in and through the "window." Attach enough pages to match the number of pictures to the bottom of the window frame. Children can flip the pages and view their movies as they read the captions they have written or dictated to match their pictures.

Main idea
Written expression

I went to the beach. 1

I saw a starfish. 2

I built a sand castle. 3

Group Pictures

After completing a reading assignment, students assemble in small groups of four or five. Give them a piece of white construction paper and assign them the task of working together to complete a picture or collage which symbolizes something they learned from the story. Their group picture or collage should represent their understanding of the story concept.

Artistic expression

Comprehension

 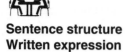

**Sentence structure
Written expression**

Main idea

**Artistic expression
Facts
Focusing**

Book Bingo

Distribute papers with eight empty blocks on each. Allow children to write the names of their favorite book or story titles, one per block. Then give them eight index cards to write a sentence about a character from their book or story. The caller reads these sentence cards. Children cover the spot that describes a book title on their bingo board. This idea can be carried out in cooperative groups, or the bingo sheets can be copied for the entire class.

Breathless

Have students read a paragraph or short story. Encourage them to tell the main idea of the story in one breath.

Get the Facts

To help children learn to distinguish the important words or facts in stories and paragraphs, highlight important facts with yellow in the book you are reading. Tell children to clap their hands when you read those lines (or touch their nose, wiggle their ears, etc.)

When they are ready to find the facts without a visual clue, read a paragraph to them. Change the pitch of your voice when emphasizing the most important facts. Ask students to model that procedure when reading to a buddy. Have them write or illustrate the most important fact that they heard or read.

Comprehension

TELLS — Fact or Fiction

Give students an acronym for reading comprehension.

T — Title. Look at the title for clues about the story.

E — Examine the story for picture or word clues to aid in comprehension.

L — Look at important words or pictures. Write down any that you think may be important.

L — Look up hard words that you may not know. Write them down or ask for assistance.

S — Setting. Identify the where and when in your reading.

Is the story real or make-believe?

Cube Review

Use an empty cube-shaped box (one a mug came in works well). Write who, what, where, and when on each side of the cube. Have students work cooperatively in teams of four. The first student tosses the cube and asks a question using the specific word which lands on top. The second student writes down the question asked. The third student answers the question. The fourth student writes down that answer. The questions may vary as well as the words printed on the cubes. Roles should rotate.

Vocabulary

Sentence structure

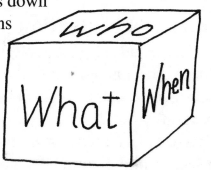

Comprehension

True or False

Label the two sides of a folder "true" and "false" or "yes" and "no." The student reads sentences on sentence strips taken from assigned readings and places them under the correct heading.

Sight words
Spelling
Vocabulary

Oral Comprehension Bingo

When reading a story to the class, prepare a grid for each child that has eight sectioned blocks. In each block, write the name of a category from the story. If you are reading a story about birds, one of the categories might be "homes." When you say the word "nest" from the story, students write that word in the box that has "homes." The first student or team to complete the grid can be the teacher's assistant for an upcoming activity.

Homes Nest	Boys	Girls	Blue Things Sky
Pets	Toys	Games	White Things

Artistic expression
Sentence structure
Written expression

Story Concentration

Each student or team member receives two large index cards. On one card, students draw a picture from their favorite class story. On the other card, a student (or team) writes a sentence to match the illustration. All cards are placed face down, five to a row in random fashion. Children turn over a description and attempt to match it to an illustration.

Comprehension

Pocket Phrases

Glue library pockets on a folder. Write who, what, where, when, and how on the pockets. Cut apart sentence strips from a story. Children match the phrases with (and place inside) the correct pocket.

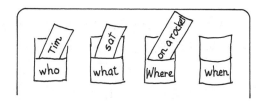

Newspaper Detectives

Students match headlines to given newspaper articles. Or, cut the headline off a newspaper article and glue the article onto a 5" x 8" index card. Students read the article and write or state their own headlines. They then flip the card over and compare their headlines with the original.

As a variation, have students cut out a headline from a newspaper article and paste supporting statements underneath to reinforce the main idea. Students may also illustrate main ideas or specific events from the newspaper selection.

Artistic expression
Main idea
Oral language
Self-assessment
Written expression

Play Corners for Interpretation

After completing a story, label one corner of the room "agree" and another "disagree." State simple interpretations from the story and instruct students to go to the corner which represents their feelings about the statement. Once the group is assembled, students explain to someone else why they agreed or disagreed. ("In the story *Ira Sleeps Over* (Houghton Mifflin, 1972), Ira is afraid to express his true feelings. Do you agree or disagree? Go to your corner and be ready to explain why.")

Oral language

Comprehension

Decoding
Oral language
Vocabulary
Written expression

Wheel of Fortune

Allow students to write down key words or ideas from assigned readings. Use these ideas to make a Wheel of Fortune game. After the class participates in the fun, keep the student-generated ideas for the test you may have to give.

For example: After reading *Naomi Knows It's Springtime* (Boyds Mills Press, 1993), one child might write "another word for ice cream." Another child guesses alphabet letters to fill in the word "custard."

Main idea
Oral language
Written expression

Translation Writing

Develop a mini-group lesson to convert the required reading to a more comfortable level. Children who read at a variety of different reading levels should be included in this group. Read a paragraph or two to the group. Encourage group members to make a readable digest of the necessary material by stating the main idea of the selection in their own words. Type or write what they say. Share copies of the revised edition with the group. The students then rewrite the material you need to teach in their own words. Keep a copy for next year's class or to share with colleagues.

Comprehension

Most Wanted

Use the same format as seen in the local post office. Have students draw a picture of the most wanted character from a story and write a description of that person.

Artistic expression
Written expression

Mapping a Story

Use a story map to improve comprehension. A blank map may be placed on an overhead or chart. Students are asked to complete the basic questions, then apply those responses to more difficult comprehension questions. Map outlines might include who, where, when, identify the main problem, the goal, the actions needed to reach the goal, and the final outcome. For some students, the teacher may need to model using the map in a mini-lesson and work toward the goal of students independently completing their maps. Some students may need to complete a map by using questions from a tape or by having a buddy fill in their blanks. This technique is often used during the reading process, allowing students to fill in as they go along. (See story map examples on pages 67-69.)

Mapping can also help students think about and plan their writing.

Organization
Written expression

For other comprehension activities, see:

"Story Map"

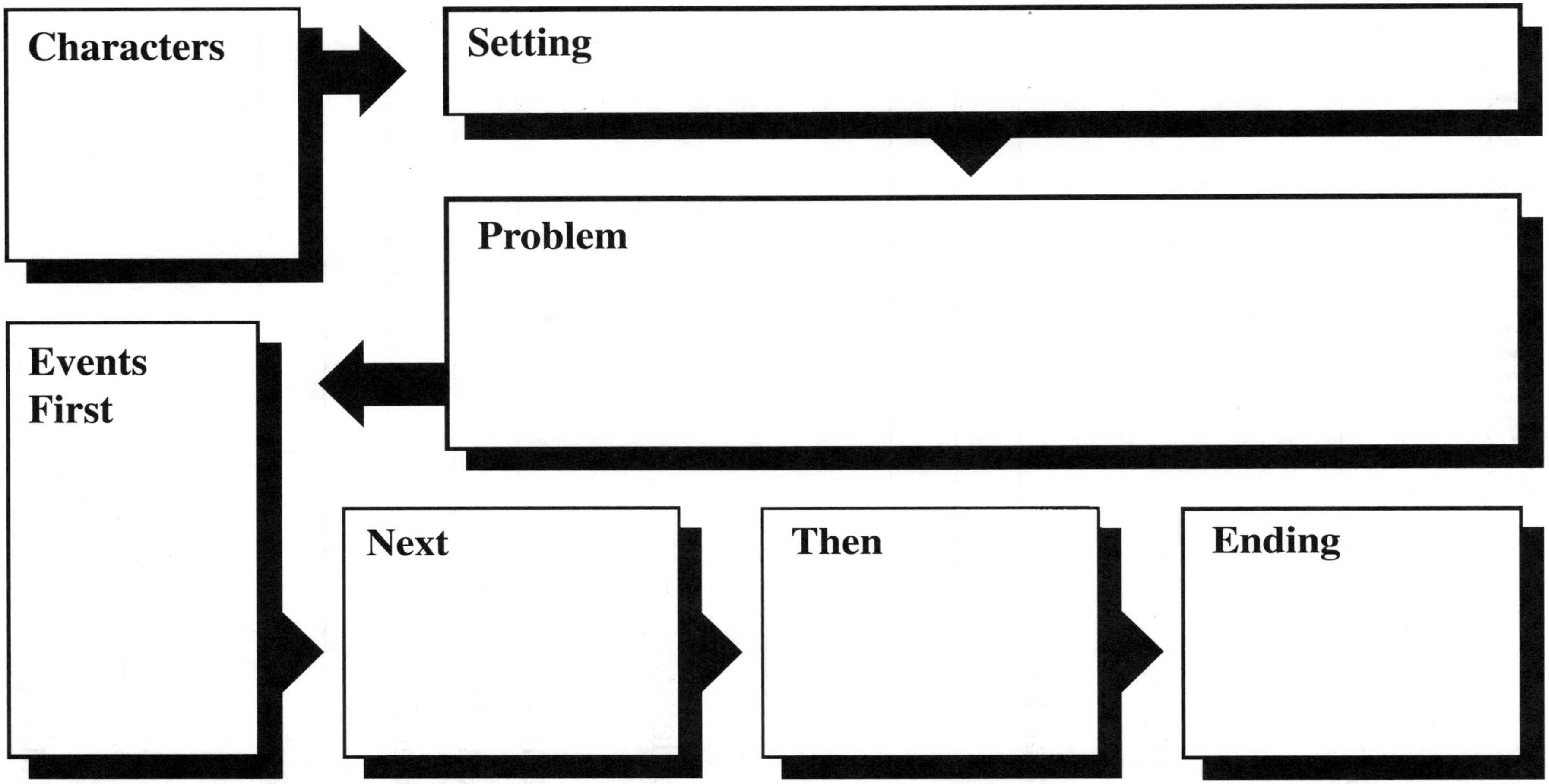

Characters

Setting

Problem

Events
First

Next

Then

Ending

"Story Map"

Title: _____

Setting:

Characters: _____

_____

_____

Problem:

Event 1 _____

Event 2 _____

Event 3 _____

Event 4 _____

Event 5 _____

Solution:

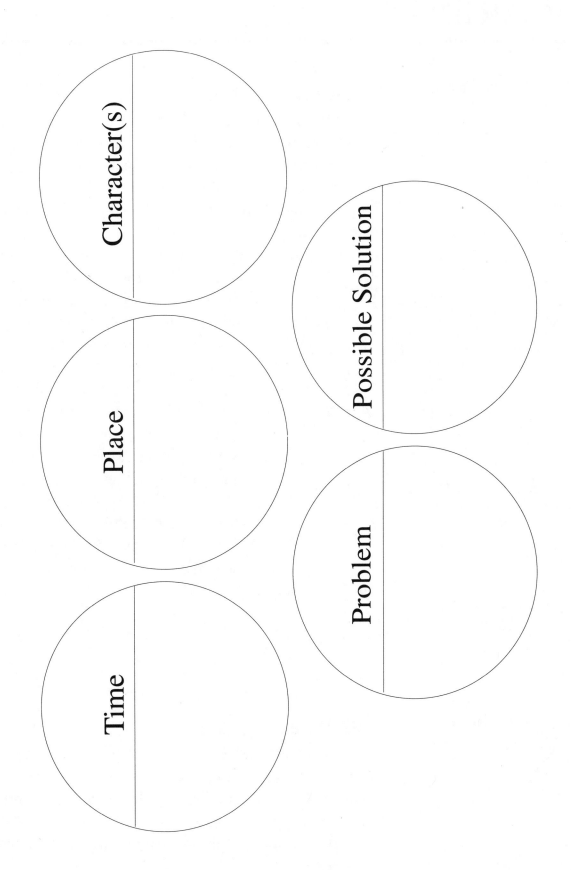

Decoding

Letters/sounds

Handful of Decoding

Teach children the five-finger approach to attacking unknown words. Display a reference chart in the room for all children to use on an as needed basis. The chart should have an outline of a hand. On each finger, give children rebus clues for word attck. Teach the steps in a jingle for easier recall. Many teachers teach this skill to the tune of "Bingo." (Bleep, frame, sound it out, then you may ask for help.)

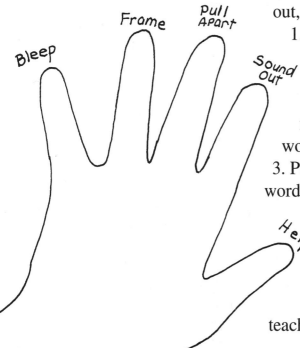

Bleep

Frame

Pull Apart

Sound Out

Help!

1. Bleep — Look at the rest of the sentence for context clues while saying bleep inside your head for that given word.

2. Frame it — Using two fingers, make a frame around the word. Study only that word to see if you can tell what it is.

3. Pull it apart — Look at the structure of the word. Does it have a prefix or suffix? Can you divide it into syllables?

4. Sound it out — Attempt to pronounce the letter sounds.

5. Help! — At this point, the student may seek help from a dictionary, peer, or teacher.

Letters/sounds

Birthday Candles

If students are unable to quickly sound out phonetic words, write those words on a cutout birthday cake with candles on the top. Help students sound out the words by blowing out the candles. In one breath, the student looks at the word and blows out the letter sounds.

Drip Drop

Place two laminated raindrops in front of the student. On the drops, write a beginning and ending consonant and leave a space between the two. Slowly drop a vowel raindrop in between the beginning and ending sounds and ask the child to say the word as the rain falls.

Toss the Dice

Cut 26 2-inch foam rubber dice by using upholstery foam and an electric knife. Pair specific letter combinations in a Ziploc bag. Students toss the dice and form as many words as possible.

Blender Fun

Draw an eight-inch arrow in thick permanent marker on an acetate transparency strip. The learner moves his/her finger along the arrow and blends the letters together as read. For example, if the word is bag, the student slowly blends the letters as read.

All in the Family

A house can be drawn on a large sheet of paper with the family name on the door (for example, at).

The windows on the house can be made so they open up to reveal a member of that family (cat in a window, bat in a window, fat man in a window, rat in a window, etc.)

Decoding

**Letters/sounds
Word families**

Wheels of Fun

Word families may be taught in a variety of ways. Often children who have difficulty with reading and decoding respond best to the word family method.

Make word wheels so only the initial consonants are changed. This is an excellent strategy for sound blending. Use two circles made of oaktag, one smaller than the other. As the child rotates the top circle, s/he forms different words.

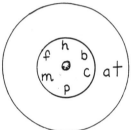

**Letters/sounds
Sight words
Spelling**

Multisensory Reading

A multisensory approach is successful with many students. Encourage them to look at a given word while noticing letters, using configuration clues, and looking for small words within big words.

They can trace specific words in sand, Jell-O, or glitter glue while noticing how it feels.

Have them close their eyes and visualize how the word looks and is used in a sentence.

They can say the word to themselves and listen for letter sounds or syllables.

Line 'Em Up

Give the student three cards with one letter on each. Ask the student to line the letters up correctly to form a sensible word.

For other decoding activities, see:

Rug Reading, p. 52   Check-up Checkers, p. 94
Wheel of Fortune, p. 64   Reading Maintenance, p. 99
Can It, p. 77

Environmental Print

"I Can Read!"

Develop with children a list of 110 things they can read. When a child becomes discouraged and says, "I can't read," share some of the things s/he can read such as baseball cards, bumper stickers, gum wrappers, candy bars, cereal boxes, eye charts, clothes labels, money, road signs, T-shirts, credit cards, etc.

Sight words

Cereal Books

Use ordinary empty cereal boxes which are commonly known to children. Laminate the box fronts and bind them into a book. Watch children "read" their first book. Younger children love to read the small cereal boxes they have chosen. This skill is transferred to Big Books and used with large cereal boxes. (The activity could be tied into eating healthy breakfasts or graphing which cereals have sugar.)

Graphing
Sight words

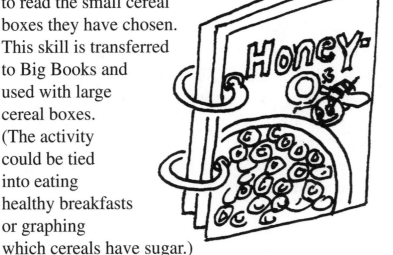

Folder Books

To develop interest in reading with children who do not truly read, give them a toy catalog or magazine. Encourage them to cut out any words or logos they can read. Paste these words on the inside of the folder to make their first reader. Allow them to share this folder book with friends and families.

Sight words

Fluency Strategies

Impress Method

The student reads aloud while the teacher reads out loud with the student, but at a slightly faster rate. The student follows along with the pointer finger. Continue for five minutes without asking any comprehension questions.

Focusing Tracking

Fluency Flashlights

Purchase a small squeezable flashlight or two for classroom use. When a student lacks reading fluency, track along the written page with the flashlight, holding it close enough to create a small ray of light. The student's eyes follow the light for reading.

Focusing Tracking

Window Boxes

Use index cards to assist students with tracking words or eliminating extra stimuli from their reading books. For young children, a window or slit cut from an index card works well.

A piece of oaktag with a box cut out of it may help the learner focus when the teacher uses an overhead projector.

Focusing Tracking

Envelopes

Use discarded window envelopes from bills for tracking. The tracking window is in place and no extra work is needed.

Allow students to use clear rulers or markers to keep their place while tracking along the printed word.

Goal Setting

Self-assessment

Individuals can develop their own goals for reading and writing. Document progress through conferencing and portfolio selections.

Name _____

Date _____

Goals for semester   1   2   3   4
READING   WRITING

Please list two goals you would like to work on this semester. I will choose the third one for you.

1.

2.

3.

Signed _____

....

Goal completion

1.   Date _____
   Comments
2.   Date _____
   Comments
3.   Date _____
   Comments

Teacher _____
Student _____

Letters/Sounds

 Consonants

Grid It Up

Consonant sounds can be practiced by gluing pictures on small cards. Place the cards on a grid where each square has a consonant letter that corresponds to the beginning sound of the object on the card.

Masking Tape Letters

Form large letters on the floor with masking tape. As a peer tutor holds up a picture, the student walks on top of the beginning letter of the picture word.

 Sight words

Sewing Letters/Words

Cut a 12" x 18" piece of poster board into the shape of the letter or word to review or learn. Punch holes in the center or along the edge and have students sew the letter or word shape.

 Letter formation

Identify by Touch

Ask students to close their eyes. Give them a specific cardboard, wooden, or plastic letter shape. Have children identify each letter by feeling its shape.

Sound Books

Students develop notebooks for their sounds. As sounds are presented on a tape or in a small group, they can cut out magazine pictures of objects that begin with each sound and glue the pictures onto the correct letter page.

Can It

Take two empty 35mm film containers. On one write the family name (op). On the other container, write letters such as c, h, t, b. The child holds both containers in a fist-like grip. The left hand rotates the letters as the child clicks the containers and sounds out the words. Children enjoy the motion, the noise, and the word attack skill.

Decoding Word families

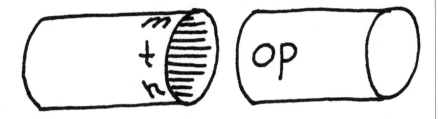

Vowel Books

Students who have difficulty with vowel sounds can make their own vowel dictionaries, using a small tablet or pages stapled together. They write a vowel at the top of each page and paste a sample picture of its sound next to the vowel. Encourage students to cut and paste pictures from magazines that contain that sound.

Vowels

"Compacting" Letters

Collect empty compacts from class mothers or from your friendly make-up counter. Glue a picture representing the sound a letter makes and how one's mouth should look on the inside of the compact. Glue the letter on the outside of the case. Students say the letter, open the case, look at the mouth formation, and self-check in the compact mirror. The correct mouth and lip formations are available from the district speech and language consultant.

Self-assessment

Letters/Sounds

Alphabet
Sentence structure
Sight words
Spelling

Alphabet Cereal

Give students who need extra help with letter recognition a small bowl of alphabet cereal. Instruct them to match letters that are the same. Then have them find someone else in the room who has those letters. Some children can place their letters on a paper plate and see if they are able to match a word in their word bank or one from the board. Children may work in teams or pairs to see which words they can form. The fun is in the eating at the end. (Anyone who has "the" may eat it, etc.)

Alphabet pasta could also be used.

As a variation of this activity, students can make as many sensible phrases or sentences as possible. (Silly sentences or phrases could also be a goal.)

Catch If You Can

List the vowels or consonants that have been studied on a chart. Have children stand in a large circle with one child in the center. The child in the center tosses a ball to a child in the outside circle as s/he calls out one of the letters displayed. The child catching the ball has to say a word containing the letter that has been called out.

Self-assessment

Hear It, Check It

Make a tape recording of 20-25 words. Instruct the child to listen to each word and write the sound s/he hears at the beginning. Answers can be given at the end of the tape for self-checking. The teacher provides a sheet, numbered to correspond with the tape, for the child to write his/her responses.

Kinesthetic Vowel Helpers

Vowels

Dramatizing short vowel sounds is very helpful to some students.

a — aaaaapple (Hold a paper apple over your head.)

e — eeeelephant (Hold an elephant trunk in front of your face.)

i — iiiiigloo (Jiggle a paper igloo over your head.)

u — uuuuugh (Hook fingers together in a clasp. Shape arms as a U with these fingers clasped. Gently hit your stomach while grunting u-u-u-u.)

o — awwww (Shape your mouth and lips into an oval shape. Trace your mouth with your pointer finger. Use your finger to pretend it is a tongue depressor and say awwww.)

Sound Boxes

To help children learn letters and sounds, have them collect empty shoes boxes for the letter of the week. Children then put real objects in the box to represent that sound.

Easel Letters

Paint a large outline of the letter of the day on a classroom paint easel. As children arrive, encourage them to cut a picture out of a magazine which begins with that letter and glue it on the easel outline. If there's no easel available, simply cut a large letter out of paper and have children decorate their letter of the day with pictures.

Letters/Sounds

Sight words

Connecting Letters and Sounds

Many children are unable to connect a symbol for a letter to an abstract sound. In order to facilitate this process, teachers may need to build the bridge for transfer. Encourage children to use symbols for the letter representations. When teaching the letter "f" for example, have children make a fat f. Then have them glue feathers on the f while emphasizing the f sound. Tell children that the f got fat from feeding off a flock of feathers. Provide time for children to take a large cutout of the f and cover it with feathers. Make f's for the children on the chart while they make the sound. Draw pictures of the f as it gets fatter. This process may be completed with other letters and picture clues.

Use the same process when teaching difficult sight words. Teach the word "see" while writing it inside eyes. Teach "big" while making the word appear bigger than other words.

Math facts
Oral language
Reading
 comprehension
Spelling

Yarn Ball Review

Have the children sit in a large circle. Start with a yarn ball and these directions: "When I toss the yarn to the first person I will say a letter. That person has the job of saying a word which begins (or ends) with that letter." Then that child holds onto the end of the yarn, says a letter and tosses the yarn to the next person. This activity can be used to review math facts, spin a story web, or check spelling.

Paint Bags

This procedure can be used for tactile reinforcement of identifying and writing letters, words, numerals, and math facts. Use a large freezer Ziploc bag. Place two tablespoons of bright finger paint inside. Zip the bag shut and reinforce the outside edges with heavy duty masking or duct tape. Children use the bag like a magic slate. They can practice writing, reading, and erasing letters, words, numbers, or math facts with soft

hand pressure. Children may use a cotton swab for writing. Stress to children who have a difficult time taking care of supplies, that everyone gets his/her own bag and needs to be responsible for its maintenance.

Letter formation
Letter recognition
Math facts
Number
  recognition
Numeral formation
Reversals
Sight words
Spelling

Helping Hopscotch

Cover a rectangular table with a clear plastic table-cloth. Draw a hopscotch shape. Place pictures cut out of magazines or workbooks in each box. As the child plays hopscotch with a plastic doll or teddy bear doing the jumping, s/he must identify the picture as well as the initial, medial, or ending consonant sound.

Consonants

For other letters/sounds activities, see:

Prefixes/Suffixes

Focusing

**Oral language
Sentence structure
Vocabulary**

Word Endings

When children have difficulty with word endings, highlight a specific ending on the page they are reading. For example, using a yellow marker you may highlight all the "ings" and bring visual attention to that suffix.

Flip Charts

To reinforce suffixes, use a white 5" x 8" index card and write the suffix on the right-hand side of the card. Using different colored 3" x 5" cards, write a root word on each. Hook the two sets of cards together at the top with word rings or within a spiral binder. Encourage students to flip the root words over while keeping the ending intact. Words can then be defined or used in a sentence.

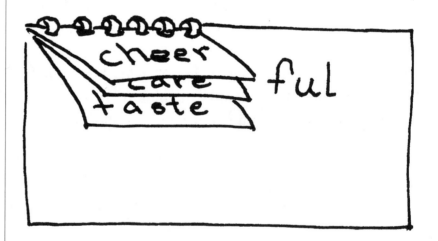

For another prefix/suffix activity, see:

Check-up Checkers, p. 94

Reversals

Reversals in Reading

Letter formation
Spelling

At the beginning stages of reading, reversals may merely indicate a lack of experience with letters and words. Teachers must decide if the reversals are merely a normal developmental stage or if they indicate a problem. Most reading/writing reversals should disappear by the end of second grade. Observe students interacting with print. Concentrate on one letter at a time. Trace the reversed letter or word on a large card, or trace felt letters. Underline the first letter. The student writes the letter or word and says it while writing. S/he traces the commonly reversed letters or words in the air, on a friend's back, or in Jell-O.

Play word bingo. Have students match the word from the teacher onto their game board.

Print a commonly reversed word on an index card with large crayons. Allow the student to repeat the word after you. The student traces the word and says or spells the word without looking it.

Place a star or green dot over the first letter of the commonly reversed word to emphasize where to begin.

Reversals in Writing

Focusing
Tracking

To prevent students reversing words when they write, place a green light on the left-hand side of the student's paper and a red light on the right-hand side to cue the child where to start and stop. Some teachers prefer to do this by putting red and green dots on a student's desk instead of on each paper.

For other reversal prevention activities, see:

Read My Mind, p. 36   Only U Smile, p. 126   Fistful of B's and D's, p. 127
Paint Bags, p. 81   Rainbow Letters, p. 126

Sentence Structure

 Oral language

What Did You Say?

Encourage children to refine their listening skills. One child says a sentence about what s/he did yesterday. Call on someone to repeat the last word said and then the word said before that. Start a sentence and stop before reaching the end. Allow children to predict what your final word or thought may be.

Word Puzzles

Children can put word puzzles together to get a better understanding of how to put words together to make sentences.

Sentence Cubes

Take six one-inch wooden cubes. Place them on the table and write one word on each to make a six-word sentence. Flip the cubes to a new side and write another sentence in a different colored ink. Once all cubes have words on each side, encourage children to shake the cubes in a coffee can and see if they can assemble the cubes to make a sensible sentence.

 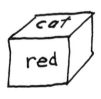   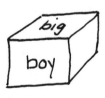 

Sentence Structure

Flip 'Em and Mix 'Em

Use a piece of 5" x 12" oaktag for a backboard. Punch three holes in the top, three inches apart. Use 3" x 5" index cards to write parts of a sentence on each. (Illustrations may be used for emergent readers.) Punch holes in the top of the index cards and hook through the top holes on the backboard. Children flip different cards to mix and match parts and make different sentences together.

Match-Ups

Artistic expression
Sequence

After students have read or listened to an assigned text or poem, make phrase cards on sentence strips and have them match these strips directly onto the original text.

Or, write specific sentences on strips of paper and have students illustrate their assigned sentence. Assemble the strips to make a new story.

Scrambled Eggs

Following directions

Prepare sentences which have words in scrambled order. Students must unscramble the words so they are in the correct order. Divide children into teams and give one set of identical cards face down to each team. Each team member draws a card. On a given signal, children turn the cards over and arrange themselves in the correct order.

Sentence Structure

**Organization
Written expression**

Writers Club

Provide graphic organizers to help students who cannot generate their own writing. Use a chart like the one below for sentence structure. Children choose a word or phrase from each section and construct a sentence.

☺	△	☻	◈
Aimee	cat	chases	the
Marian	mouse	starts	a
Haz	car	eats	an
Diane	bone	saw	this
Ryan	dog	kept	
Jan	ice cream		

○　　▢　　◇　　△.
Haz　eats　this　ice-cream.

Punctuation

Jeopardy Punctuation

Place sentences on sentence strips. Do not place any punctuation at the end of the sentences. Have students work in pairs or triads. After reading their sentences, students must state the needed punctuation. (Following the format of the television game show, all answers are given in the form of a question, for example, "What is a period?" "What is a question mark?")

For other sentence structure activities, see:

Book Bingo, p. 60
Cube Review, p. 61
Story Concentration, p. 62
Alphabet Cereal, p. 78
Flip Charts, p. 82
Crossing the Creek, p. 90
Vocabulary Detectives, p. 91
Game Fun, p. 92
Ring Toss, p. 92
Missing Words, p. 92
Fishing for Fun, p. 95
Sandwiching Flash Cards, p. 98

Sequence

Sequence Spinner

Use the concept of two circles on top of each other with a wedge cut out of the top one. Have five or six wedges outlined on the circle underneath. Instruct children to write the most important events from the story. When the top circle is attached with a brass brad, children can share a piece of the pie with a friend, detailing the sequence of events.

Reading comprehension

Fishy Stories

After reading a story, present children with the outline of a fish body. Have vertical bone lines drawn on the inside of the fish. Encourage children to write the main ideas from the beginning to the end of the story on each of the bones.

Reading comprehension Main idea

Strippers

Write an event from the story on each of three sentence strips. Allow children to manipulate the sentences and place them in the correct order. Children may work alone or in teams. Strips should be numbered in sequence on the back for self-correcting.

Reading comprehension Self-assessment

Step It Up

Upon completion of a reading selection, distribute three, four, or five strips of paper with a specific story event written on each one. The strips should be made in varying sizes so they can be assembled in descending order of steps from first to last.

Reading comprehension

The girls got mad.
The dog ate the cake.
They made a cake.
The girls had a party.

For other sequence activities, see:
Student Choice, p. 53   Match-ups, p. 85   Picture This, pp. 120-121

Sight Words

Pop-up Flash Cards

Using the same format used to make pop-up books, make flash cards more exciting by presenting them in pop-up fashion. Write the word to learn on the outside and have a pop-up picture on the inside for reinforcement.

Directions for pop-ups:

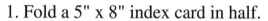

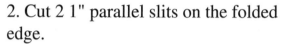

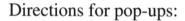

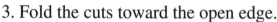

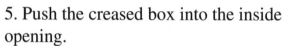

1. Fold a 5" x 8" index card in half.
2. Cut 2 1" parallel slits on the folded edge.
3. Fold the cuts toward the open edge.
4. Crease.
5. Push the creased box into the inside opening.
6. Open to pop up.
7. Write the word to learn on outside, glue picture inside.

Letters/sounds

Make and Take

Write a student's name (or a word to practice) on the board. Take away one letter while the student looks away. Have the student guess what is missing and replace that letter.

Blast Off

Make a ladder or rocket ship blast-off pad and place a sight word on each level. The child pronounces words to see how far s/he can get.

Sight Words

Bingo

Put pictures of sight words like ball, cake, truck, or car on one side of a card. Write the word on the other side. Make a game board similar to a bingo card with each sight word written on it. Give one to each child. Cards are placed with the word side up in a pile. The child must be able to say the word correctly before placing it on his/her board. The picture on the back makes the game self-correcting.

boy	in
cake	on
top	girl

Tape Talk

A teacher or an at-home parent volunteer reads a list of 10 given sight words on a tape. The student follows along and points to the words as they are read. Immediately after this follow-and-point activity, the tape gives the words in context and has the listener point to the word in a sentence. Next the tape says a word and gives a specific direction to the listener involving that word. "Find the word 'talk' on the list. Put a triangle over the word 'talk.' Now find 'boy.' Draw two lines under the word 'boy.'"

Following directions

Card Snatch

Put sight words on large cards, giving all but one child a card. Children hold up their cards. The teacher calls out a word and if the child without a card finds it, s/he takes the card.

89

Sight Words

Letter formation
Self-assessment

Casper's Message

Write a new word of the day on the chalkboard. Invite a student to carefully use a pointer finger to trace over the word. As it is traced it will also be gradually erased, but part of it will remain barely visible. Have students close their eyes and try to see what the word looked like before it turned into Casper the Ghost's writing. Invite children to attempt to write the word in the air or on a piece of paper. In order to self-correct, have another child come to the board and trace over Casper's message with chalk.

This activity can be adapted to help with letter formation. Give children letters or words with missing parts. They must write the correct part to complete the letters or words.

Quick Eyes

Hold up a card with the word of the day printed on it. Allow children to study it for 30 seconds. Remove the card. Challenge children to find the word hidden anywhere else in the room, in their newspaper page, on their own worksheet, or in their books.

Oral language
Sentence structure
Vocabulary

Crossing the Creek

This game can be used with pairs or triads. Place new vocabulary words on individual pieces of 8" x 11 ½" paper. The student then spreads these papers out on the floor face up. The goal is for the student to say each word and use it in a sentence as s/he steps on it while attempting to get across the creek.

Dominoes

Review words in a domino game by writing a word on half of an index card and placing a picture, not the matching picture, on the other half. The children lay out the cards and build off one another in domino fashion.

Language Masters

Language Masters provide a tactile/kinesthetic approach to learning for students. These machines can be purchased through audio/video supply catalogs. To use a Language Master, students are given a blank card and dictate one word they want to learn for the day to a peer. The word is written on the card. The child sees the word. The tape/record button is pressed on the Language Master. The child says the word into the recorder. The child picks up the card, places it in the magnetic slot, says the word, hears the word repeated on the recorder, and then removes the card. Children see the word, touch the card, hear the word, and say the word all in a matter of seconds.

Vocabulary Detectives

The student or peer tutor writes new vocabulary from the completed reading on individual 3" x 5" index cards. Place five words at a time in front of each child. Give clues to describe the new word. The child must say the word and use it in a sentence. "Can any detectives in here find a new word that means 'scared'?" The student picks up the word "terrified" and uses it in a sentence.

Oral language
Sentence structure
Vocabulary

Sight Words

Oral language
Self-assessment
Sentence structure
Vocabulary

Missing Words

Four known sight words are written on the board. Students read the words and use them in a sentence. One word is erased while the students cover their eyes. They guess which word is missing and use it in a sentence. The word is then put back on the board for self-checking.

**Following
  directions**
Oral language
Sentence structure
Vocabulary

Game Fun

Make a game board on oaktag with a path of squares. Start and finish squares are marked with directions like "move ahead three squares," "move back three squares." The board space is limited. Words that are to become sight vocabulary words are written in the open squares. Students take turns tossing dice. When they land in a square, they must pronounce or use that word in a sentence in order to remain in that space.

Oral language
Sentence structure
Vocabulary

Ring Toss

Use a chart-size (24" x 36") pegboard and attach curtain hooks or large pegs where index cards can be hung. Write vocabulary words on the index cards and hang the cards from the hooks. Give the student a rubber jar ring to toss at a hook. Remove the card from the hook where the ring landed. The student must read the word and use it in a sentence.

Rhyme

Riddle Rhymes

Riddle rhymes are used to reinforce new words or review old ones. Students hear statements on tape (or by having someone read to them) such as, "I rhyme with boy. You play with me. I am a _____ (toy)."

Sight Words

Pocket Reading

Use a heavy-duty manila envelope. Cut out a two-inch window. Now write six words or letters to be reviewed on a 2" x 10" strip. Push the strip through the window and read to a partner.

Focusing
Letter recognition

Back Writing

Students work in pairs for this activity. Student one is given a set of cards containing letters, numerals, sight words, or spelling words. Student one slowly traces the number, letter, or word on number two's back. Student two must identify what has been traced.

Letter formation
Letters/sounds
Numeral formation
Numeral recognition
Spelling

Slap Jack

Purchase a set of blank, laminated playing cards. Write the words or sentences to be reviewed on two identical cards. Mix the cards and deal them out equally to two children. Students play the game like slap jack, turning over one card after another in sequence. When two identical word cards are exposed face up, the first one to call out that word or sentence takes the entire pile. The first student to collect all the cards is able to earn extra time at the computer or time to volunteer as a peer helper.

Glitter Words

Children who need tactile reinforcement can write sight or spelling words with glitter-glue pens. Or, they can mix bright glitter with white glue and use the glue bottle as a pencil.

As a variation, they can write their words in white glue and sprinkle glitter on the glue before it dries.

Letter formation
Spelling

Sight Words

Compound words
Decoding
Letters/sounds
Prefixes/suffixes
Vowels

Check-up Checkers

Make checkerboards on oaktag with alternating two-inch black and red squares. Laminate. When students understand the game concept of checkers, use the alternating red squares to reinforce specific concepts. (Long A words, compound words, prefixes or suffixes, etc., are written on the red squares.) Before a player can land on a square, s/he must identify the word.

Rummy

Choose eight or ten sight words to reinforce. Write the words on index cards or blank playing cards. Put each word on four different cards. Deal five cards to each of the two or three players. Place the remaining cards in a pile with one facing up. Students draw a card from either pile while attempting to match sets of four like words. When a set is made, the student displays it face up. The first person to be out of cards is the next dealer.

Self-assessment

Ladders of Fun

Cut learning ladders out of construction paper or oaktag. Encourage students to write new words that they have mastered on each rung of the ladder until all are filled. Children keep track of their own progress and compete only with themselves.

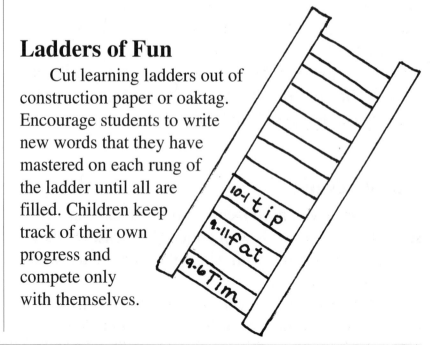

Let's All Show

Pass out identical packs of sight words to students in small groups or to the class as a whole. The teacher or teaching assistant calls out a given word and all pupils hold that word up against their foreheads.

Fishing for Fun

Attach a paper clip to a paper fish. On one side of each fish, write the new word(s) for the week. Attach a magnet to a string on a dowel. Invite children to fish for words. They must read the words they catch or use them in sentences.

Oral language
Sentence structure
Vocabulary

Word Lists

(adaptations for teachers who are required
to test by word lists)

Sight words must be meaningful to readers. Many students are more successful if sight words are presented in categories instead of random listings. Words are classified on color-coded index cards and presented to learners, as in the following example:

- on white index cards — color words, such as blue, orange, yellow, red, and green
- on blue index cards — connector words, such as because, but, and, with, also, and too
- on yellow index cards — talk words, such as said, tell, shout, ask, and call
- on pink index cards — the "no way" words, such as don't, never, no, not, and won't

Sight Words

Team Spirit

Words are listed on the blackboard. Two students stand or sit with their backs to the lists. As the teacher calls out the word, the students turn around. The first one to find and identify the word receives a point. Team help is permitted.

 Focusing

Flagging a Word

Make an oaktag word flag and attach a handle. When sentences are flashed on the overhead, use the word flag to pull words in and out of context. For a more permanent word flag, use a butcher block cutting board or an acrylic cutting board with a handle. Spray with fluorescent paint from the hardware store and use this to lift words in and out of context on the screen.

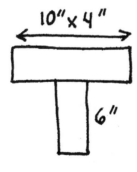

10" x 4"

6"

Concentration

Make two sets of cards, one set having pictures of sight words and the other having the words written out. Spread the word cards face up. Place the picture cards face down. Students look at the first word card. The first student to match the picture to the word collects both cards.

Sight Words

Pocket Folders

Using a pocket folder, students can write on the left-hand pocket "Words I know" and on the right-hand pocket "Words I am learning." Individual word cards are then transferred from one side to another.

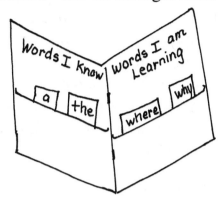

Word Rings

Give students silver notebook rings. The words they need to review can be slipped on the ring. Stars are affixed to the upper left-hand corner each time the student reads the word correctly. Three stars and the word comes off the ring.

Word Necklaces

Students wear the word of the day around their necks on a large string. Each day a new word is attached to the word necklace. At the end of the week the necklace is worn home.

Word Banks

Take a photo of your town or city bank. Make copies for each child on card stock. Glue these real photos onto a 6" x 9" manila envelope. As children learn to read or write new words, they can deposit the word cards in their banks for future reference.

Sight Words

Oral language
Sentence structure
Vocabulary

Sandwiching Flash Cards

Many students are required to learn words by using flash cards. When giving students cards to work with, begin by working with only 10. Sandwich the known with the unknown words to ensure success in the following manner: three known words, one unknown, two known, one unknown, two known, and one unknown. Share this stacking technique with parents and aides. Have the student say each word, define it, and use it in a sentence.

For other sight word activities, see:

Film Flam Film, p. 30
Screen Boards, p. 41
Water Painting, p. 42
Overhead Math, p. 42
Word Pockets, p. 51
Oral Comprehension Bingo, p. 62
Multisensory Reading, p. 72
I Can Read!, p. 73
Cereal Books, p. 73
Folder Books, p. 73
Sewing Letters and Words, p. 76
Alphabet Cereal, p. 78
Connecting Letters and Sounds, p. 80
Paint Bags, p. 81
Shaping Letters, p. 128
Label Spacers, p. 130
Toothbrush Spelling, p. 135

Reading Maintenance

This makes an excellent reference chart to be displayed in the classroom for all children to use as needed.

If I become confused — I need to read more to see if it gets better.

If I want a preview of what's to come — I need to speed ahead and skim for information.

If my brain is overloaded — I need to take a breather, read more slowly, and make notes.

If I hit a brick wall with a word — I should skip it, sound it out, or look for visual clues.

If I lose my train of thought — I should put on the brakes and retrace my steps.

If I need help — I should look the word up in a dictionary, ask a friend, or ask the teacher.

Decoding
Organization
Reading
** comprehension**

Silent Reading

To help students read silently without whispering, ask them to lightly place their "shh" finger to their lips. This makes students aware of lip movement while reading.

My Own Dictionary

Encourage children to keep a dictionary of words they need for reference. Included in this should be a page of direction words such as "circle," "underline," and "cross out" along with visual examples.

Spelling
Vocabulary

Study Skills

Organization
Reading
comprehension
  Facts
Self-assessment

Recalling Facts Read

Teach students the RCRC method of reading and retaining information. This makes a handy reference chart.

R — Read. Read a small part of the material. Read it again.

C — Cover. Cover the written material with your hand or paper.

R — Retell. Tell yourself what you read.

C — Check up. Lift the paper and check to see if you remember it.

Organization
Reading
comprehension
  Facts

Notable Facts

Give students who need help writing facts a paper divided into two sections. Students write the most important facts they heard or read on the left-hand side of the paper. Instruct them to write only brief key phrases or words in this portion. When they complete their reading assignment, they write the details on the right-hand side that match the facts they previously wrote.

large meat eating dinosaur	T. Rex
spike on his tail	
flying reptile	

Study Skills

How to Answer Questions

When teaching students how to answer written questions from specific material, teach these quick steps:

1. Read the question. (For example, "What is the capital of Pennsylvania?")

2. Turn the question into part of your answer. (The capital of Pennsylvania is...)

3. Say or think of the answer in your head. (Think about the Pennsylvania map or visualize the list of five capitals you had to learn.)

4. Complete the answer. (Finish the answer with Harrisburg.)

Organization
Reading
 comprehension

Workable Worksheets

Give children worksheets to simplify studying. An example of this strategy might look like this:

Page 33 — The main idea for Chapter 2 is in the second paragraph. Locate it and write it in your own words.

Pages 35-40 — Skim this section quickly. We will see a video that explains this next week.

Page 41 — There are three sentences that support the main idea of this chapter. Write them in your own words.

Page 42 — Read slowly! This is the meat of the entire chapter.

Reading
comprehension
 Main idea
Workbooks/
 worksheets
Written expression

Study Skills

Organization
Reading
  comprehension
Self-assessment
Written expression

QAD

Divide a paper into thirds. On the left-hand (Q) side of the paper, have the student write questions they have about the assigned reading or questions they want to have answered. In the middle (A) section, they write answers they have found to those questions. On the right-hand (D) portion, they write supporting details from the story.

Reading
  comprehension
Self-assessment

Process Reading Strategies

Before reading, encourage the child to skim the story and look at the pictures. Set a purpose for reading. Have the child think about what s/he can tell you about the story. Ask him/her to predict what will happen in the story.

Invite the child to create mental pictures while reading and to feel the mood of the story and characters. Say, "Does what you are reading make sense? Stop yourself and reread anything that doesn't make sense. After reading, ask yourself what you just learned. How does this fit with what you knew before beginning? How will you use this new information? Retell this to a friend or use a tape recorder to retell the story."

Focusing
Organization
Spelling

Banks

Provide sentence or word banks for children to refer to when answering specific questions. Many children know the answers but are unable to process the spelling needed in order to fill in given blanks (see pages 122-123).

Study Skills

Outlining

Teach older students how to outline the material they have read or will write about. "On-line Outline" on pages 112-113 helps students who need a starting place for outlining.

Organization
Reading
  comprehension
Written expression

KWL

This strategy is used to model the thinking necessary for reading while actively involving students with the printed word. Give students (or teams) paper divided into thirds. Place K on the left-hand third, W in the middle, and L on the right-hand third of the paper. Instruct students to write everything they know about the topic under K and everything they want to know about it under the W section. After completing the reading or unit, students write everything they've learned under the L section. This strategy lends itself well to thematic units as well as reading.

Organization
Reading
  comprehension
Self-assessment
Written expression

K	W	L
Jim has a pet.	How can I be a vet?	Pets are hard work.
Dogs are fun.	What do you feed pet lizards?	Being a vet is like being a doctor.
Tara is allergic to cats.	How many teachers have pets?	All k-2 teachers in this school have a pet.
Pets need care.		

For example: "We are going to begin a unit on pets. Write down all you know about pets and what you want to learn." The L (learned) column can be used for students to assess what they have learned as a result of their study.

For other study skills activities, see:

Highlighting Texts, p. 13
On-line Outline, pp. 112-113
Find It, Define It, pp.116-117
From Abstract to Concrete, pp. 118-119
Picture This, pp. 120-121
Location Stations, pp. 122-123

Written Expression

Clear It Up

Have students take a blank piece of paper. For one minute, have them write down everything that is on their minds. This allows students to clear their minds so they can begin to concentrate on the writing process.

Budding Writers

Pair children so they can dictate stories or journal entries to a partner who will write the information down.

Oral language

Flip Frames

Flash a slide or a wordless frame from a filmstrip on the screen. In one minute or less have the children write down what is happening in the picture. Children with slower processing may need more time, or they may give verbal responses.

Main idea

Caption This

Encourage students to write captions or several sentences from candid school photos taken throughout the school year.

Story Enders

In place of story starters give students story enders. The goal is for students to build a story around a particular ending.

Written Expression

Gerbil Diary

Send home a diary with the class pet (or with a stuffed animal mascot). Encourage students and their families to document the visitor's adventures in their home.

Webbing

Graphic organizers (see pages 106-110) help some children feel at ease before beginning the writing process. They can also help children make sense of their reading.

**Organization
Reading
comprehension**

For other writing activities, see:

The Web

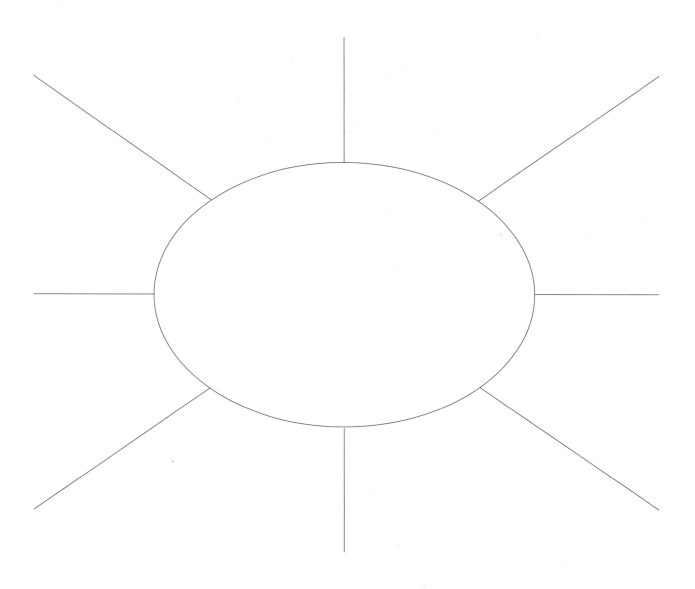

Name: _____

Feelings Web

Story Title

Feeling

| When? | | When? |
| Why? | | Why? |

Name of Character

| When? | | When? |
| Why? | | Why? |

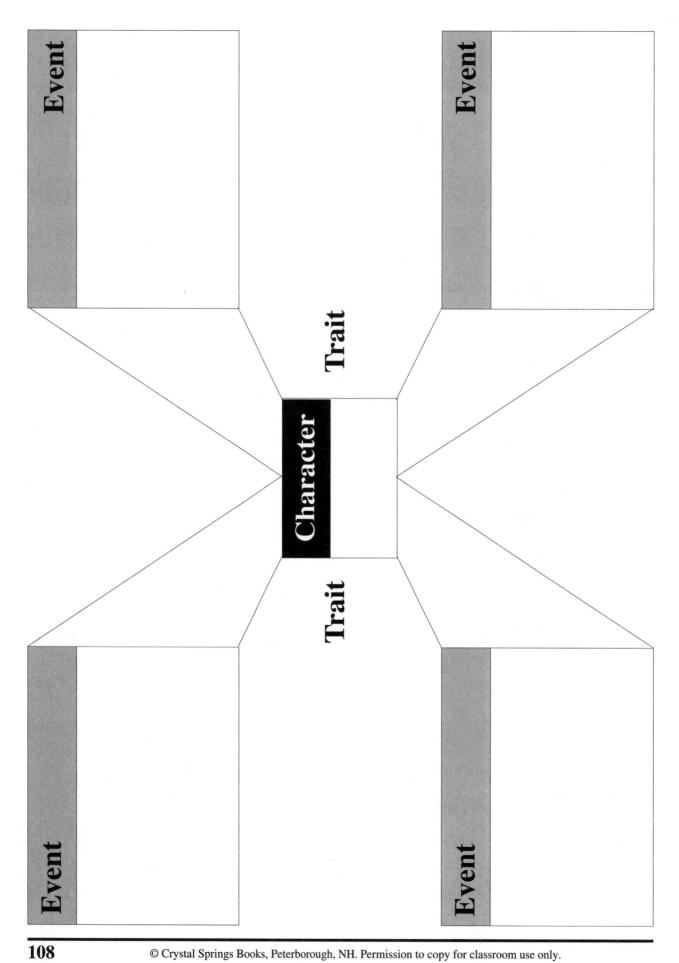

Details

$+$

Main Idea

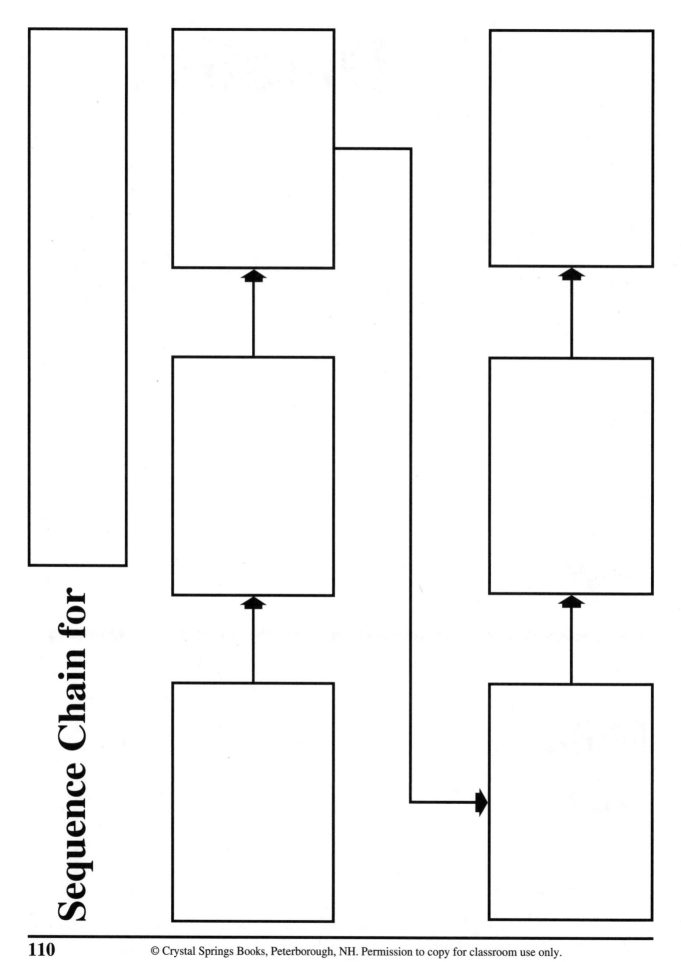

Sequence Chain for

Sample Adaptation

On-line Outline

WHO: Used by students who are unable to organize, outline, study, or write successfully. It is also for those who have difficulty focusing or staying on task.

WHAT: An adaptable outline used to record vital information and assist student with locating major points of interest.

WHERE: Incomplete or pictorial outlines are presented on an overhead or directly in front of the student for reference.

WHEN: Used to review learned material or rehearse new topics for discussion.

HOW: Major topics or subtopics may be presented using cloze or first letter clues.

WHY: Records highlighted information or used to review for a test. Decreases the amount of written work needed and any note taking.

On-line Outline
Social Living

I. Firepeople (p. 51)

    A. Work at _____

    B. Drive a _____

    C. Help by _____

II. Policepeople (p. 58)

    A.

    B.

    C.

III. Postal Workers (p. 64)

    A.

    B.

    C.

Sample Adaptation

Putting It to Work

WHO: Used by students who learn through the tactile, kinesthetic approach of hands-on learning.

WHAT: Posters, collages, pictures, letters, interviews, projects, or models are used to put presented, learned knowledge to work.

WHERE: Freedom to move throughout the room in small groups and pairs enhances the application of knowledge.

WHEN: Used in place of tests, term papers, writing assignments, and to develop cooperative groups.

HOW: Provides hands-on, higher level application of learned information.

WHY: Encourages peer support and group interactions to facilitate putting facts to work in real-life situations.

Putting It to Work
Social Living

Step-by-Step Planner

1. Make a family album, a group picture, a clay model, or hand prints from your family.

2. Write one sentence about each member.

3. Draw what your final display will look like.

```


```

Be ready to share your final project on _____ .

Sample Adaptation

Find It, Define It

WHO: Used by students who are unable to find necessary words and definititions, or those with weak memory or handwriting skills.

WHAT: A structured setup of words and descriptions from stories or chapters to aid in categorizatons and explanations.

WHERE: Headings and bold face clues are taken from chapters or readings which are necessary for understanding new concepts and categorizing facts.

WHEN: Used to improve memory and decrease need for handwriting while locating information in a chart form.

HOW: Terms are arranged by topics and listed on specific charts by categories. Page clues are used for individual or group clues.

WHY: Simplifies definititions, categories, and finding key words.

Find It, Define It
Reading

Directions — Illustrate each new word from your story.

(p. 51) Caleb	(p. 52) sandwich
(p. 53) jar	(p. 54) packing

Sample Adaptation

From Abstract to Concrete

WHO: Used by students who need assistance with comprehension and relating abstract facts to visual, concrete images.

WHAT: A visual aid or organizer used to illustrate an abstract thought or concept.

WHERE: An abstract idea which is read or discussed is brought to a concrete level using pictorial clues, symbols, or a framework on paper.

WHEN: Used to review old information, rehearse new information, and bring learned material to a concrete focus.

HOW: Pictures, graphs, symbols, and organizational tools focus on concrete thinking.

WHY: Motivates students to relate new information on a personal level, enhances abstract vocabulary, and provides visual assistance for memory.

From Abstract to Concrete
Hands-on Writing

Put the ice cream scoops together to make a sensible cone.

the fat man

was

eating

hot dog

a large

Sample Adaptation

Picture This

WHO: Used by students who have trouble listening to stories or lectures, organizing information, comprehending written words, or locating information.

WHAT: Information is presented in charts, graphs, or pictures.

WHERE: Charts, word banks, visual clues, and page numbers are pictured on sheets to assist with large blocks of learned material.

WHEN: Used to help students draw conclusions, relate cause and effect, sequence events, demonstrate relationships, and organize material.

HOW: Charts, graphs, timelines, calendars, or word banks are used to tie visual clues to auditory presentations.

WHY: Simplifies studying; eases review; aids in comprehension, relationships, sequencing, and locating information.

Picture This

Whole Language/Timeline

Read the story, *If Once You Have Slept on an Island* and fill in the timeline.

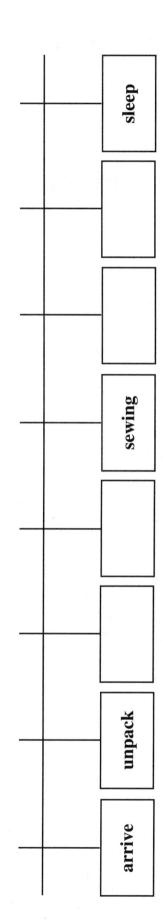

arrive | unpack | | sewing | | | | sleep

by Iris Rynbach, Caroline House, Boyds Mills Press

Sample Adaptation

Location Stations

WHO: Used by students who are unable to organize information, those who have difficulty remembering what was read, or those with handwriting deficits.

WHAT: A structured format to aid in reading for meaning and locating pertinent information.

WHERE: Subheadings or text page clues help students find key topics or vocabulary in written materials.

WHEN: Used as a chapter review, a rehearsal prior to a lesson, as a study aid, a lesson summary, or as an independent assignment.

HOW: Open-ended statements are used with pertinent information deleted. Cloze procedures, lists, or definitions are also employed.

WHY: Simplifies recollecting information, locating information, and reading grade-level texts.

Location Stations

Reading/Trade Books

Word Bank

shabby	Mudge	dirty
happy	TV	excited
		washed

1. One night Henry and his father were watching _____ .

2. The cat Henry found was very _____ .

   This word means very _____ .

3. Mudge was very _____ and _____ .

4. The cat loved _____ .

5. The cat_____the dog.

Henry and Mudge and the Happy Cat, by Cynthia Rylant. Bradbury Press

V. Handwriting Adaptations

General Strategies

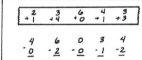

- Check the student's seating to make sure s/he can see the board.

- Check vision.

- Enlarge copy forms.

- Place work to be copied on student's desk rather than on the chalkboard or chart.

- Decrease the amount of work to be copied.

- Use highlighting tape to focus on what is to be copied.

- Place writing paper on a slant board for writing or on a closed ring binder on the slant for correct wrist positioning.

- Place two wooden blocks under the front two desk legs to slant the entire writing surface.

- Allow student to use a word processor.

- Allow for short written answers rather than detailed written responses to questions.

- Allow more time for student to complete written work.

- Provide direct and quick feedback to written work.

- Use high-interest words for handwriting practice.

- Use erasable pens instead of pencils.

- Children who have difficulty with muscle control may benefit by having a wrist weight placed on their writing hand as a reminder of correct wrist placement on the writing surface.

- To help children develop fine motor skills: have the child hold a paper clip in his/her nondominant hand and link a second clip to it with the dominant hand. The child continues until there are 10 in a row. Give the child a yardstick and a box of thumbtacks. The student pushes one tack into every inch on the stick.

- Use a chalkboard to help children develop gross motor writing skills.

Formations

- Tape record letter formation ("O begins at the middle line, circles toward the left, closes at the line").

- Use desk top letter charts for formation cues.

- Go from simple to complex letter formation.

- Write on graph paper with each letter in a box.

- Check pencil grip.

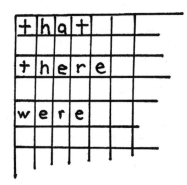

Paper

- Allow students to skip lines when writing.

- Use colored glue to differentiate lines on paper.

- Use markers to color code lines on writing paper.

- Place a strip of masking tape on desk to cue student for correct paper position.

Letter Formation

Letter recognition
Numeral formation
Number recognition
Reversals

Rainbow Letters

Use different colored crayons to trace around letters which are difficult for students to form. The student should start tracing the designated letter with yellow, next blue, and finally red. (This activity can also be used with numerals.)

The rainbow letters can be used for a colorful bulletin board or to hang from the lights.

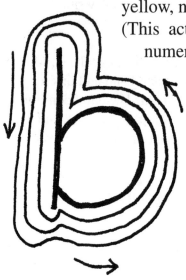

Letter recognition

Crawling Away

Use wide masking tape to form letters on the floor. Children first crawl, then skip, and finally hop the letters. For an extra challenge, children can do cross-lateral marching around the letters by marching with the right hand and left foot swinging out together and then the left hand and right foot swinging together.

Encourage children to say the names of the letters as they move over them. Transfer the gross motor activity to a fine motor activity on paper with crayons, markers, or pencils.

Reversals

Only U Smile

Provide a visual representation to show that u's smile. This lessens confusion between u and n.

Letter Formation

Listen to the Rhythm

Some teachers are successful using a metronome to help children develop the smooth pace of the writing exercise. (Note, some children who are easily distracted will not be able to concentrate with the metronome.)

Tracing Trackers

Letter recognition
Numeral formation

Have students practice letter or numeral formation by first placing a piece of acetate over a letter. They trace over the paper model onto acetate. Then they trace on tracing paper which has been placed over this model letter. Finally, they copy the letter, numeral, or word onto a paper placed next to the written work.

Dot-to-Dot Writing

Have beginning writers learn to write their name, letters, or words by connecting the dots. Eventually the number of dots are decreased until no dots are needed.

Fistful of B's and D's

Teach students how to make fist models of b's and d's. Encourage peer partners to trace each other's fist and place models on individual work spaces. This strategy is used to prevent reversals.

Letter recognition
Reversals

Letter Formation

Wallpaper Writing

Cut the letters of a student's name out of wallpaper samples. Glue the name onto a piece of oaktag. Have the student place a piece of newsprint over the letters and do a letter rubbing with crayons over his/her name. Next, have the student trace the name with eyes open, then closed. Finally, the student attempts to write the name with the model close by.

Letter recognition
Letters/sounds
Sight words
Spelling

Shaping Letters

Use pipe cleaners, wikki sticks, clay, or play dough and have the child form letters and words. Give the child a large cutout of the letter or sound for the day and have the child cut magazine pictures out that begin with that sound. Or have the child cut out that particular letter from the daily newspaper.

As a variation of this activity, use frozen bread dough. When thawed, give each child a golf-ball sized piece of dough. Have children practice shaping a letter, their names, or a sight word. They can then bake and eat the letters or words.

Following directions

I Am Thinking Of

Have children fill in or identify missing parts of a given letter. For example, say: "I am thinking of a letter that has one line going straight down on the left, one line across the top, and one line across the middle. What letter is it?" The children follow these auditory directions and form the marks on their papers to make the letter.

Letter Formation

Overhead Cursive

To help children make the transition to the smooth movement of cursive writing, use the overhead projector to model how to make smoke trails coming out of an airplane.

Or, teach the children to string beads on paper.

Make curls on a head.

Make waves to jump in.

Board Writing

Spelling

Have children develop gross motor skills by writing on white boards or chalkboards in large, full arm strokes. Thick paintbrushes, sponges that have been cut in half and dipped in clear water, or moistened envelope sealers can be used to write on chalkboards.

If you have children who suffer from asthma, use white boards and unscented dry markers. Your local hardware store can make white boards by cutting white shower boards into appropriate sizes for the classroom.

Children can also practice their spelling words using these materials.

Letter Formation

Organization

Letter Size and Spacing

Boxed-in Writing

Cut a window box out of cardboard or an index card. Use the boxes to practice specific letter writing. This box guide helps children know how to correctly place their letters. For many children, it is advantageous to color code the box to match the line of the writing paper.

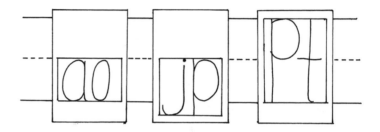

Organization
Sight words
Spelling

Label Spacers

Give students a variety of sizes of address labels. Assign words to be written. Have students judge which word will best fit into which label size. The same skill can be applied to different sized envelopes. This adaptation is most helpful for children who cannot place words on their paper with correct spacing or consistent size.

For other letter formation activities, see:

Screen Boards, p. 41
Canvas Charts, p. 41
Water Painting, p. 42
Overhead Math, p. 42
Human Alphabet, p. 52
Identify by Touch, p. 76
Paint Bags, p. 81
Reversals in Reading, p. 83
Casper's Message, p. 90
Back Writing, p. 93
Glitter Words, p. 93
Toothbrush Spelling, p. 135

Pencil Grips

Sock Grippers

Have students bring a white athletic sock to school. Place the sock on their writing hands. Cut two small holes for the index finger and thumb. This is now where the student's thumb and finger should come out and correctly grip the pencil. Children love having visitors in the classroom think they all have casts on their arms!

Golf Grips

Place a pencil inside the holes of a wiffle golf ball. The golf ball provides the student with a relaxed grip on the pencil.

Putty in Your Hands

Place a small ball of silly putty or clay around the pencil for correct gripping position.

Adaptations for the Physically Challenged

Allow the child to use stencils and letter templates for tracing. Individual name cards can be made by taping together stencil letters in the student's name.

Some children may need to have individual rubber stamp letters taped together to form their names. They are encouraged to stamp their papers.

Many children enjoy using a label maker for their names (or spelling tests).

Magnetic letters can be placed on cookie sheets to form words and names.

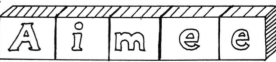

VI. Spelling Adaptations

General Strategies

- Students who have difficulty with spelling choose 5, 10, or 15 words to be tested on, depending on their individual needs. All students take the test together and attempt all words, but certain students are graded only on their "chosen few."

- Give oral spelling tests. Use peer partners or parent volunteers to assist.

- Use materials other than pencil/paper. Take spelling tests in dry Jell-O, shaving cream, or finger paint.

- Practice by writing words in black crayon and then finger tracing these words.

- Allow student to use a word processor.

- Use tape recorded spelling reviews.

- Have student supply missing letters to words already printed on test or fill in only the missing vowels.

- Color code vowel patterns on list. Find and use spelling patterns.

- Unscramble the letters of the spelling words on the test instead of writing from memory.

Spelling Activities

Anagram Reviews

Have students write spelling words vertically. They must write another word next to each letter of that word.

Configuration Spelling

Trace the outline of spelling words on the student's paper. The student will then fill in the correct letters by matching the configuration.

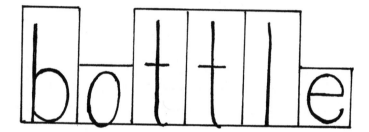

Configuration Bingo

Use the same idea as above, except have the configuration of six or eight words written in designated blocks of a bingo card. The teacher holds up or says a spelling word, and children cover that configuration shape on the bingo card.

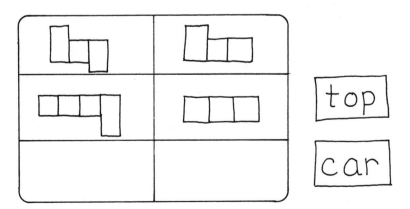

Spelling Activities

Word families

Self-assessment

Cookie Spelling

Gather small cookie sheets or metal cookie can lids. Give the student magnetic letters that form the word family for spelling. Have him/her add or change only the necessary beginning letters on the tin. The teacher can check words as s/he circulates, or a peer can check the spelling.

Flashlight Spelling

Give students small penlight flashlights and have them stand up behind their chairs. Dim the lights. The teacher dictates a spelling word and children "write with the light" on their desks.

Letter Tiles

Gather letter tiles from discarded Scrabble games. Have students manipulate the tiles and build correct spellings.

Look-Say Spelling

Have the student orally repeat the word after you, then follow these steps:

- Look at the word. Notice its shape and spacing. Trace it.
- Spell the word to yourself, to a peer, or on a tape recorder.
- Write the word while you see it.
- Cover the word and try to spell it.
- Check yourself.

Spelling Activities

Stampede Spelling

Provide the student with the necessary foam letter stamps to form the week's words. Next have the student stamp out the spelling word on large paper while others write.

Toothbrush Spelling

Have four or six large toothbrushes and paint at the paint easel. Have the children practice writing their spelling words in paint using the brushes and large white paper.

**Letter formation
Sight words**

Vowel Clues

Give students spelling test papers with the vowels already placed in the words. Students then build the words by placing consonants around the vowels.

**Consonants
Letters/sounds**

For other spelling activities, see:

VII. Behavioral Management

Many times the gray-area children in our classrooms experience difficulty completing tasks, obtaining daily goals, and feeling successful.

The following forms can assist any or all children with building self-esteem, meeting a contract, reaching goals, organizing themselves, monitoring individual progress, building positive home-school relationships, and developing friendships.

Pages 138 through 140 should be used to help young children set their own goals in behavioral and academic settings. The younger the child is, the simpler the goals should be.

When working on goals with children, keep in mind that they need to be given one obtainable goal and remain with it until they achieve success for at least three consecutive days. For some children, the day may need to be broken into morning and afternoon sessions. A child or teacher may place a smiley face or sticker in the blanks next to the goal to show success. The ultimate goal is to have the child monitor his/her progress and take responsibility for determining if s/he achieves the goal.

"The ultimate goal is to have the child monitor his/her progress and take responsibility for determining if s/he achieves the goal."

Name _____   **Name** _____

Week of _____   **Week of** _____

Mon.				
Tue.				
Wed.				
Thurs.				
Fri.				

	Free Choice	Clean Up	Recess
Mon.			
Tue.			
Wed.			
Thurs.			
Fri.			

My Goals

My Goals

Name: _____ Date: _____

My goal(s) this week:	Monday	Tuesday	Wednesday	Thursday	Friday

Name: _____ Date: _____

My goal(s) this week:	Monday a.m.		Tuesday a.m.		Wednesday a.m.		Thursday a.m.		Friday a.m.	
	a.m.	p.m.	a.m.	p.m.	a.m.	p.m.	a.m.	p.m.	a.m.	p.m.

Daily School Report for _____
Date _____ My overall behavior today was:

| appropriate | appropriate |
| inappropriate | inappropriate |

Goal:

Comments:

Please describe specific follow-up at home:

	Comments		Comments
Art	**APPROPRIATE**	**INAPPROPRIATE**	
Gym	**APPROPRIATE**	**INAPPROPRIATE**	
Music	**APPROPRIATE**	**INAPPROPRIATE**	
Library	**APPROPRIATE**	**INAPPROPRIATE**	
Computer	**APPROPRIATE**	**INAPPROPRIATE**	
Cafeteria	**APPROPRIATE**	**INAPPROPRIATE**	
Recess	**APPROPRIATE**	**INAPPROPRIATE**	

Parent signature

_____'s
Morning to do list

To Do	Yes	No
1. Things in the closet		
2. Lunch chart		
3. Get a chair		
4. Get books		
5.		

_____'s
Morning to do list

To Do	Yes	No
1.		
2.		
3.		
4.		
5.		

_____'s
Afternoon to do list

To Do	Yes	No
1. Empty mailbox		
2. Put things on desk		
3. Pack backpack		
4. Coat, hat, gloves, boots		
5. Go to front carpet		

_____'s
Afternoon to do list

To Do	Yes	No
1.		
2.		
3.		
4.		
5.		

Once the goal has been reached, congratulatory sheets keep families posted on progress. Children use these forms to set independent goals and to choose their own rewards.

No kidding . . .

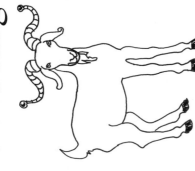

You'll be pleased to know that

has reached the goal of

today in school.

Don't be baaaa-shful,

this deserves an extra hug.

Signed

Add one more stripe . . .

has reached the goal of

today.

Signed

My start to finish goals are:

My prize will be _____.

_____
Student

_____
Parent

_____
Teacher

A win-win deal for you:

If _____

before _____

Then _____.

_____ _____
Child   Teacher

_____ _____
Principal   Date

Contracts are a more structured approach to help children set goals and meet behavioral or academic standards.

Assisting With a Contract

1. Select one or two behaviors at a time.
2. Describe the behavior(s) in observable terms.
3. Jointly decide on rewards for motivation.
4. Write contracts in clear language or pictures.
5. Gather data.
6. Review daily.
7. Rewrite if contract is unobtainable.

Choosing a Behavior

1. Where does the behavior occur?
2. How often does the behavior occur?
3. When does it *not* occur?
4. What usually happens when it does occur?
5. What happened immediately before the behavior occurred?

Writing a Contract

1. Be specific about the goal — "Do my math work in class." — "Hand in my homework before 9 a.m."
2. State when the goal is to be reached — each day, during rug time, once a week.
3. Jointly decide on a specific reward — "Will be allowed to read two books to kindergarten." "I will receive 30 extra minutes in the computer lab."
4. Detail when the reward will take place — during school, at lunch, at home.
5. Keep reward in line with expected behavior.

Assignment Contract

Name _____ Grade _____

Subject _____ Date _____

I, _____ agree to complete the following classroom assignments for

_____ by _____ .

Assigned Work	Due Date	Satisfactory Completion
1. _____	_____	_____
2. _____	_____	_____
3. _____	_____	_____

Student _____ Date _____

Parent's Signature _____

I, _____ agree to reward _____

with _____

for satisfactory completion of all listed assignments.

Teacher _____ Date _____

Student Contract

Name _____ Date _____

I, _____ promise to

for _____ days/weeks.

In return my teacher

will _____

_____

_____ .

If I do not keep my promised goal, I will _____

_____

_____ .

Student _____

Teacher _____

Parent _____

145

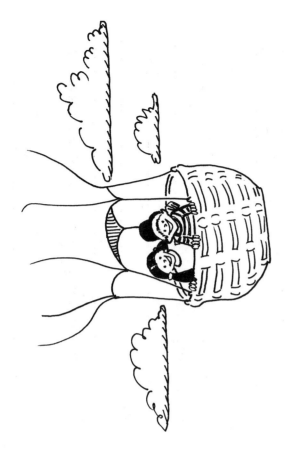

Just dropping by to tell you what a great friend _____ is.

This was demonstrated today by _____

_____

_____ .

Lucky friend _____ Date

Good friends can receive a pat on the back for their support by using the following forms. Each child should receive recognition for friendship and kindness at least once a month.

Helping Hand Award

For lending a helping hand to a friend

_____

you have earned the right to

_____

146

Parent Newsflash!!!

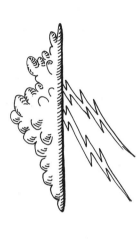

Dear _____ ,

You will be proud to know that your child _____ is now working on _____ in the classroom.

We could use your help at home with _____
_____ .

If you have any concerns or questions regarding this information, please list them and return this form to the classroom. All of us thank you and appreciate your time and effort.

Signed _____

Date _____

These forms are used to open home-school relationships. Nothing makes caregivers happier than receiving good news about their child. The ultimate goal for all teachers should be to send a positive note to each child at least every 10 days.

This no "tail" we're telling...

This medal of honor is being given to _____

because _____
_____

on this _____ day of _____, 19 _____ .

Officer in charge _____

Parent Communication Sheet

Name _____ Date _____

Teacher(s) _____

Time/Subject	Behavior was appropriate	Effort was put forth	Homework was completed
	Total	**Total**	**Total**

M = Most of the time
S = Some of the time
N = Not at this time

Reinforcement _____

Consequence _____

Will be sent _____ daily _____ weekly

Daily (or weekly) classroom performance forms inform parents of classroom performance and work habits.

Teacher's Response Form

Name _____   Date _____

Activity	On Time Y N	Correct Y N	Neat Y N
	Total	Total	Total

My Daily Plans

Student Name _____

Teacher(s) _____

Directions: Fill in each row of this form as you complete each assigned activity and then check with your teacher.

Today's Date	What I Need To Do	How Long It Took	How Well I Did	What I Need To Do Next

Tickets applaud children's efforts with positive attention. These two pages of tickets can be easily cut apart and distributed.

Reward Tickets

Wow!_____ has earned _____ from our Reward Board by earning _____ points by _____ .

Don't forget: You've earned the privilege to use _____ for earning_____ points for appropriate behavior. Enjoy!

Friendship Reward goes to _____ and_____ for earning _____ points cooperatively in the class. The reward to be shared is _____ . Congratulations, friends!

Hop to it! _____has earned the reward of _____ for _____ on this_____ day of _____ 19 _____ . Way to go!

What a cool cat! _____ has chosen _____ as a reward for _____ _____ . Way to go.

Reward Tickets

You have earned _____ extra minutes
at the center of your choice_____
for your great work in our classroom.

This certificate allows_____
to read a story of your choice to our school
principal on _____ . Your hard work
has earned you this special privilege.

For your hard work you have earned _____
minutes of free time on _____ .

This allows you to have lunch with the
teacher of your choice on _____
in room _____ because you _____
_____ .

These attention-getting tickets tell children that we recognize they are seeking attention, but it is an inappropriate time.

Attention-Getting Tickets

Your behavior is telling me you need attention. Let's talk at _____ .

I'm glad you are in this room, but I cannot give you any more attention. Write me a note.

We will talk later. I need to teach right now!!!

I notice you, but I need to keep working with the whole group.

Professional Bibliography

Bradley, Mildred Odom. *The Slow Learning Child in the Classroom*. Manhattan, KS: Master Teacher, Inc., 1989.

Curran, Lorna. *Cooperative Learning Lessons for Little Ones: Literature-based Language Arts and Social Skills*. San Juan, Capistrano: Resources for Teachers, 1991.

Dunn, Rita, and Dunn, Kenneth. "Kids Must Learn How to Learn Alone." *Phi Delta Kappan* (March 1987).

Goodman,Gretchen. *Inclusive Classrooms From A to Z: A Handbook for Educators*. Columbus, OH: Teachers' Publishing Group, 1994.

Greene, Lawrence J. *Kids Who Underachieve*. New York: Simon & Schuster, 1986.

Harwell, Joan. *Complete Learning Disabilities Handbook*. New York: Simon and Schuster, 1989.

Lang, Greg, and Berberich, Chris. *All Children Are Special: Creating an Inclusive Classroom*. York, ME: Stenhouse Publishers, 1995.

Mann, Jean. *Literacy Labels* (set of six books). Columbus, OH: Essential Learning Products, 1994.

Rosner, Jerome. *Helping Children Overcome Learning Difficulties*. New York: Walker Publishing, 1979.

————. *Visual Motor Program, Auditory Motor Program*. New York: Walker Publishing, 1979.

Routman, Regie. *Invitations: Changing as Teachers and Learners*. Portsmouth, NH: Heinemann, 1991.

Vail, Priscilla. *Smart Kids With School Problems*. New York: E.P. Dutton, 1987.

Organizations/Resources

Center for Success in Learning
1700 Preston Rd., #400
Dallas, TX 75248

CH.A.D.D. — Children With Attention Deficit Disorders
499 NW 70th Ave., Suite 308
Plantation, FL 33317

Council for Exceptional Children
1920 Association Drive
Reston, VA 22091

Gateways — Pennsylvania Initiative to Support Inclusion
Western Instructional Support Center
5347 William Flynn Highway
Gibsonia, PA 15044-9644.

Learning Disabilities Association (LDA)
4156 Library Road
Pittsburgh, PA 15234

National Center for Learning Disabilities (NCLD)
99 Park Ave.
New York, NY 10016

Index